DISCUSSION PAPER 42

Examining the South Africa–China Agricultural Trading Relationship

RON SANDREY AND HANNAH EDINGER

NORDISKA AFRIKAINSTITUTET, UPPSALA 2009

Indexing terms
Foreign trade
Economic relations
Agricultural trade
Trade agreements
Export earnings
Access to markets
Comparative analysis
China
South Africa

Language checking: Peter Colenbrander
ISSN 1104-8417
ISBN 978-91-7106-643-5
© the authors and Nordiska Afrikainstitutet 2009
Printed in Sweden by GML Print on Demand AB, Stockholm 2009

Contents

List of Tables

List of Figures

Acronyms and Abbreviations

AGOA	African Growth and Opportunity Act
COFCO	China National Cereals, Oils and Foodstuffs Import and Export Corporation
EFTA	European Free Trade Area
EPA	Economic Partnership Agreements
EU	European Union
FTA	Free Trade Agreement
GTAP	Global Trade Analysis Project
HS	Harmonised System
MOFCOM	Ministry of Commerce, PRC
NTBs	Non-Tariff Barriers
PRC	People's Republic of China
PROVIDE model	Provincial Decision-Making Enabling model
RSA	Republic of South Africa
SACU	South African Customs Union
SADC	Southern African Development Community
SARS	South African Revenue Service
SPS	Sanitary and Phytosanitary
SOEs	State-owned Enterprises
TBT	Technical Barriers to Trade
TCF	Textile, Clothing and Footwear
TDCA	Trade Development and Corporation Agreement
TRQ	Tariff Rate Quota
US	United States
VAT	Value-Added Tax
WTO	World Trade Organisation

Acknowledgements

The authors would like to thank Ferdi Meyer, University of Pretoria; Cecelia Punt and Sanri Reynolds from the Western Cape Department of Agriculture; Taku Fundira, Trade Law Centre of Southern Africa (TRALAC); and Hayley Herman, Centre for Chinese Studies (CCS), University of Stellenbosch for assistance and useful comments on this paper.

The authors would also like to express gratitude to the Nordic Africa Institute for commissioning the research paper.

Foreword

In recent years, Africa has emerged as a dominant region in China's foreign policy. In early 2006, China released its first major policy paper on its relations with Africa and, in November of the same year, held an historic jamboree in Beijing with almost all African heads of state and government attending. The Beijing summit of the Forum on China-Africa Cooperation (FOCAC) adopted a declaration to continue the momentum on bilateral cooperation indicated in the China-Africa policy document earlier released by Beijing. The China-Africa policy paper highlights 30 initiatives that will be the focus of Sino-African rapprochement. Prominent on this list is the overriding Chinese interest in African raw materials and the need to cooperate with Africa in multilateral forums such as the United Nations and the World Trade Organisation (WTO), etc.

Undoubtedly, the relentless Chinese 'march into Africa' in the area of trade and investment will have an important impact on future development and poverty eradication in Africa. This is even truer at a time when efforts to establish a fairer trade regime between Africa and its traditional partners in the European Union on the one hand and at the WTO on the other are experiencing great setbacks. It is in this context that the Nordic Africa Institute in late summer 2007 requested the Centre for Chinese Studies at Stellenbosch University to conduct these comprehensive studies on the South Africa-China agricultural trading relationship.

China has boosted its trade relationship with Africa in both bilateral and multilateral forums. Since joining the WTO in 2001, China has worked closely with African countries in the context of the current Doha Development Round of trade talks. China has also collaborated with South Africa, Nigeria and other African countries as members of G20 to carve out a profile representing perspectives from developing countries at the WTO. By contrast, in terms of trade and investment, China has a trade surplus with Africa. By 2005, China's trade with Africa reached a staggering US$ 40 billion and it is estimated to reach US$ 100 billion by 2010. Breaking down this trade volume by sector reveals that imports of oil and other raw materials from Africa make up the lion's share of Sino-African trade. Through the FOCAC mechanism, the Chinese state has boosted Chinese trade and investment in Africa. In addition to having trade agreements and export credit arrangements with most African countries, China has also used tied aid to promote its investment on the continent.

In his state of the nation address in 2006, President Thabo Mbeki of South Africa emphasised the need for a FTA with China. This was in recognition of the growing volume of trade between the two countries, which in 2006 had increased over the previous year by 26 per cent By most accounts, South Africa is China's largest African trading partner. While there is a growing need among policy-makers and implementers [?] to learn more about the nature and impacts of China's broader trade and investment in Africa, it is even more imperative to understand how this trade is being conducted in a sector such as agriculture, upon which most African countries rely for their export earnings. Although these studies focus on South Africa, they give us a very clear idea of what we should expect in examining the agricultural trade relationship between China and other African countries.

Accordingly, these comprehensive studies by these knowledgeable scholars, Ron and Hannah, are very timely. As an emerging centre of economic growth in the world economy, China is striving to establish a clearer footprint in Africa than ever before. The need to understand this rapprochement has been made more acute by the current financial crisis. With its focus on agricultural trade, this well researched study uses empirical data up to the end of 2007 to provide a lucid explanation of the potential benefits of China's growing trade with Africa on South Africa's economy. The study covers China's and South Africa's positions as both importers of agricultural products from and exporters of agricultural products to each other's markets. In producing the paper, the authors have carefully analysed in a rather comprehensive manner data from Chinese and South African sources. In order to provide a rather fresh perspective in their analyses, a section has been devoted to the nature of the non-tariff barriers facing South Africa's exporters to Chinese market.

March 2009
Dr. Yenkong Ngangjoh Hodu
Nordic Africa Institute

1. Introduction

1.1 Background

Over the last quarter of a century, global trade patterns have changed dramatically. On the world scene, a major feature has been the emergence of several Asian nations as strong participants, with their growth being fuelled in part by strong US imports over this period and generally reducing global tariffs. The most recent Asian nation to steal the limelight has been China.

China has been following the pattern set by several others such as, initially, Japan, then more recently Chinese Taipei (Taiwan), Singapore, Korea and Malaysia. However, the sheer size of China and the immense potential as this nation strives to regain its place as a 'top tier' global player makes it both an enormous potential market and a serious potential competitor in third country export markets and in the home market for imports that may crowd out domestic production. Thus, there are many dimensions to the 'China factor'.

The observed evolution of China's economy is important for South Africa, which has since undergone considerable trade liberalisation of its own as the country puts the troubled years of apartheid behind it and strives for international competitiveness. It is interesting and imperative to examine the implications for South Africa of the potential convergence of the two phenomena, i.e., South African trade liberalisation and the phenomenal growth of the China's economy. In particular, does China present export opportunities for South African agricultural products, and conversely, is China a competitor to South African exports into third markets?

While China is undoubtedly much more competitive in global manufacturing export markets for products such as clothing and electronics (with automobiles poised to join these products) and is at the same time becoming a magnet for considerable volumes of raw materials such as South Africa's iron ore, the issue of agriculture also needs to be considered. It is well known that China is drawing in vast resourcvolumes of agricultural commodities such as cotton to fuel its manufacturing export boom, for example, but less is known about how the Chinese market will influence South African export commodities that do not share cotton's high profile.

1.2 Objective and Outline of the Paper

The objective of this paper is to explore what China may mean for South African agricultural exports in the future. Of necessity, the exploration of this topic covers many of the crucial facets of the current and potential relationship.

Section 1 is the general introduction to the paper, while section 2 provides an overview of the China-South Africa trade relationship with particular emphasis on agricultural trade. Section 3 describes the methodology used to analyse the trade links between South Africa and China, while section 4 provides an overview of non-tariff barriers to trade. The findings of the study are set out in section 5 and the conclusions are presented in section 6.

2. The Trading Background: China and South Africa

This section introduces the reader to the topic by providing an overview of the China-South Africa trade relationship, with particular emphasis on agricultural trade. China's trade data used in this section are sourced from the World Trade Atlas (WTA). Data for South Africa are also obtained from the WTA. In the analyses, import (rather than export) data are used wherever possible, because the data are generally more reliable.

2.1 Overview of China's Aggregate Trade

2.1.1 China's Exports

While Chinese exports to the world during 2006 were up 27.15 per cent to US$ 969,323 million, Chinese exports to South Africa increased by an even larger 50.78 per cent to US$ 5,768.8 million from the 2005 figure of US$ 3,826 million. This raised South Africa as an export destination for Chinese goods by one place on the table to 27th.

Electrical machinery (US$ 844.6 million) and general machinery (US$ 794.2 million), with increases of 57 and 46 per cent respectively, remained the top products leaving China for South Africa, but more noticeable is the dramatic increase in reported clothing exports. The third main export, knitted apparel (HS 61), increased by 138 per cent from US$ 280 million in 2005 to US$ 667 million during 2006, while exports of woven apparel (HS 62) increased by a more moderate 47 per cent from US$ 389 million during 2005 to US$ 571 million during 2006.

Figure 1: China's top exports to South Africa and annual growth rates

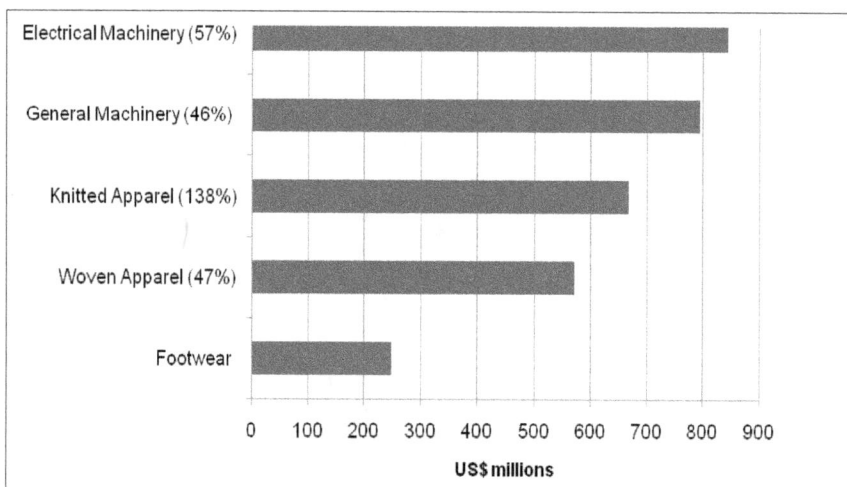

Source: World Trade Atlas (2006)

Thus, clothing exports to South Africa as measured in terms of these two HS chapters alone passed the one billion dollar mark to US$ 1.24 billion in the year ending December 2006. Given the recently imposed quotas on these imports into South Africa, it will be interesting to see if this is the high point followed by a retreat or just another milestone. Footwear, at US$ 249.8 million, was in fifth place.

2.1.2 China's Imports

While Chinese imports from the world during 2006 were up 19.9 per cent to US$ 791,794 million, Chinese imports from South Africa increased by a similar (but lower) 18.9 per cent to US$ 4,095.3 million from the 2005 figure of US$ 3,443.6 million. This lifted South Africa as a source of imports into China one place on the table to 28th.

Ores remain the top import from South Africa (US$ 1,268 million and up by 31.1 per cent), followed by precious stones and metals (US$ 1,185 million and up by 23.8 per cent).

Next was the HS 98 'special products' category (US$ 461.6 million and unchanged from 2005), followed by iron and steel products, for which imports declined by 30 per cent to US$ 298 million (we note that this decline is very similar to the global decline of 23.6 per cent in this HS chapter). In fifth place were mineral fuels, where imports surged by 248 per cent to US$ 189.5 million. Imports from South Africa remain very concentrated, with the top five HS 2 chapters continuing to contribute over 83 per cent of the total.

Figure 2: South Africa's top exports to China and annual growth rates

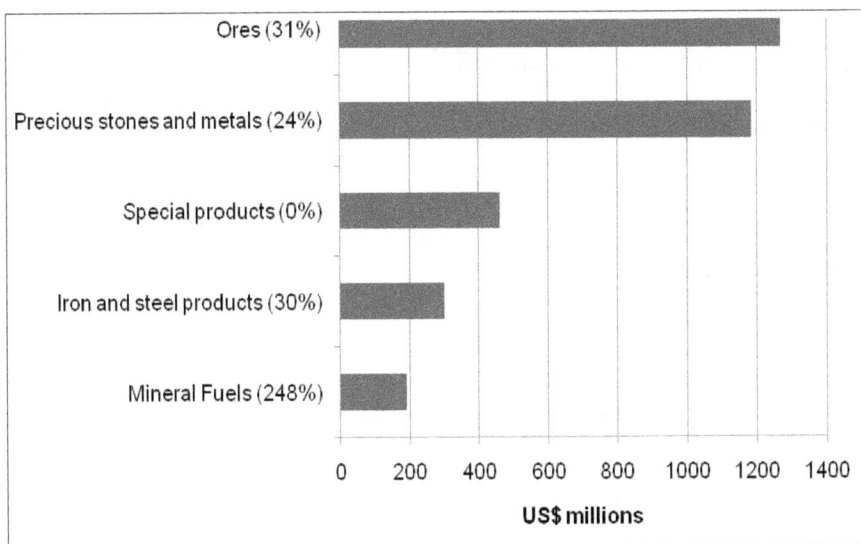

Source: World Trade Atlas (2006)

Accordingly, in the space of three years South Africa has moved from registering a trade surplus of US$ 3.46 billion through a more balanced US$ 0.38 billion to a deficit of US$ 1.7 billion.

2.2 Overview of South Africa's Aggregate Trade

2.2.1 South Africa's Exports

Overall, South African exports to the world during 2006 increased 11.62 per cent over the 2005 figure to US$ 57.9 billion, with exports to China up by a much larger 48. per cent to US$ 2,036 million from US$ 1,376 million in the corresponding period. China remains at fifth place on the South African export table, behind the EU15, Japan, the US and 'unallocated' (a category that covers exports of precious metals and stones for which the specific destination is not disclosed).

Iron ore (US$ 409 million), with an increase of 19.8 per cent, tops the list of products leaving South Africa for China. Also noticeable is the dramatic increase in petroleum products and oils obtained from bituminous material, with reported exports increasing from zero in 2004 and 2005 to second place in 2006 with exports of US$ 254 million. These were followed in turn by steel products (US$ 215 million), chromium ores (US$ 177 million), ferro-alloys (US$ 106 million) and manganese (US$ 93.5 million). The export value of each of these four products at least doubled in 2006 over 2005.

Figure 3: South Africa's top exports to China and annual growth rates

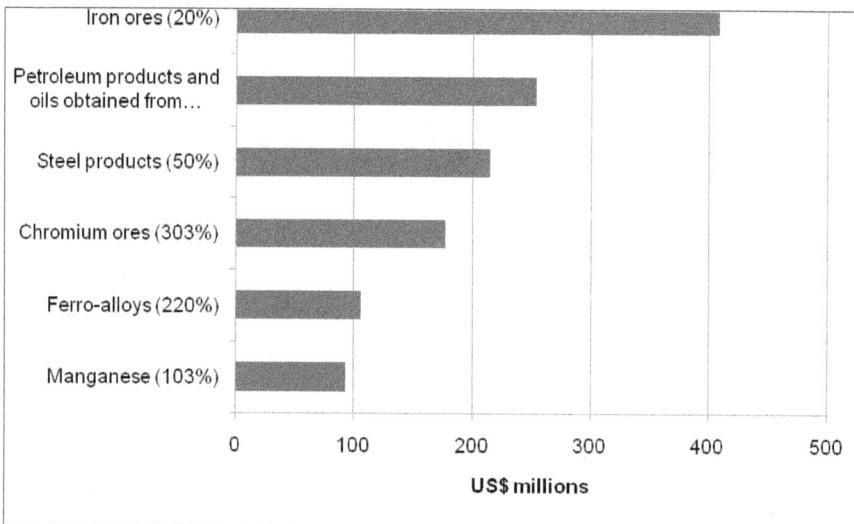

Source: World Trade Atlas (2006)

2.2.2 South Africa's Imports

Overall, during 2006 South African imports from the rest of the world were up 23.9 per cent to US$ 6,818.7 billion.

South Africa's imports from China increased by 38.4 percent, and stood at US$ 6,819 million. This increase exceeded the increase in global imports, and meant that China retained second place on the individual country list behind Germany.

The top 20 individual HS 4 import lines from China remained relatively stable from 2005, with machinery, electrical machinery and textiles, clothing and footwear (TCF) products occupying the top twelve places (and representing one-third of the total imports). Interestingly also, further scrutiny of the first 40 HS product groups reveals that only six of these 40 lines represent lines of textiles and clothing on which South Africa imposed quotas from 1 January 2007, and in these lines the increases over 2005 are tightly bunched between 31.87 per cent and 45.21 per cent (compared with the overall average of 38.42 per cent).

According to this South African trade data, the trade deficit with China of US$ -4,783 million is second only to that with the EU (US$ -5,256 million). This trade deficit had increased from US$ 2,571 million in 2004 to US$ -3,551 million in 2005. It is, however, worth noting that gold exports (US$ 5,232 million) are not allocated to specific countries, and precious metals and stones are the second main import into China from South Africa.

2.3 Reconciliation of Data on Trade between China and South Africa

A general problem with trade data is the disparity between data reported by the exporting party and data reported by the importing party. Attempts at reconciliation do not solve the problem entirely. Sandrey (2006a) examined trade flows between South Africa and China and, as part of that examination, undertook a reconciliation between South African exports and Chinese imports. This exercise revealed that, during 2005, reported South African exports were only 39 per cent of the reported Chinese import value. This result was largely influenced by a 'special category' of returned and repaired goods that were not reported as exports, by massive under-reporting of diamonds and platinum that had probably transited through a third country and a difference for iron ore that seems to be accounted for by the transport costs associated with a bulky low-value commodity.

The data in Table 1 represent an update for 2006 and confirm these general observations. It should be noted that although Chinese export/South African import data are somewhat closer in aggregate, there are differences at the HS 2 Chapter level.

Table 1: Trade data reconciliations between South Africa and China, 2006

South Africa's Data	US$ Million	China's Data	US$ Million
From RSA to PRC (exp)	2,036.0	From RSA into PRC (imp)	4,095.3
From PRC into RSA (imp)	6,818.7	From PRC to RSA (exp)	5,768.8
Deficit/Surplus	-4,783	Deficit/Surplus	+1,673
Main RSA export HS 2		Comparable PRC import HS 2	
Ores etc. HS 26	816	Rank 1	1,268
Iron and steel HS 72	336	Rank 4	299
Mineral fuels HS 27	270	Rank 5	189
Rank 10	27.4	Rank 2 precious stones etc HS71	1,185
Not an RSA coding		Rank 3 'Special' HS 98	462
Main RSA import HS 2		Comparable PRC export HS 2	
Machinery HS 84	1,453	Rank 1	845
Electrical machinery HS 85	1,259	Rank 2	794
Apparel HS 62	455	Rank 4	571
Rank 5 (behind footwear)	337	Rank 3 Apparel HS 61	667

Source: World Trade Atlas (2006)

2.4 China's Agricultural Trade

2.4.1 China's Agricultural Imports

Figure 4 shows Chinese agricultural imports over the period July-December 1996 through to January-June 2007 in six-monthly periods. The data are expressed in US$ billions on the right and as a percentage share of total Chinese imports on the left. The WTO's definition of 'agriculture' is used[1]. Imports were stable in dollar terms through to around 2002 before steadily climbing to just over US$ 16 billion, while the percentage share of total Chinese imports has been consistently around 4 per cent much of the past decade.

Figure 4: China's agricultural imports as a percentage of total exports and total exports (biannual data)

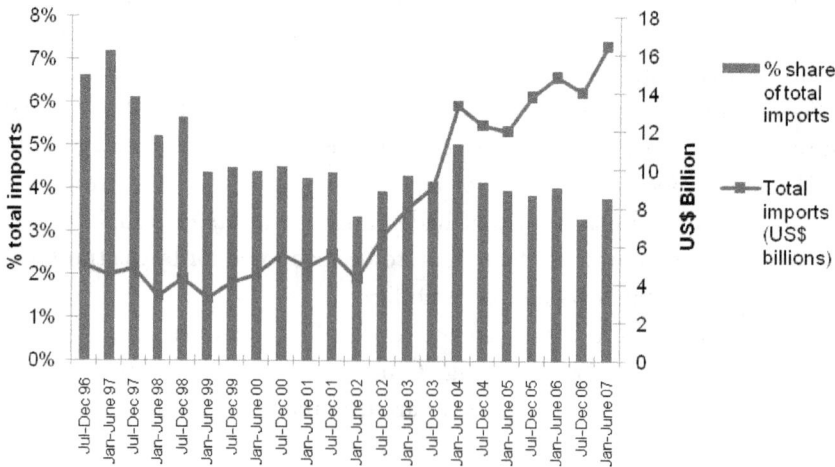

Source: World Trade Atlas (2007)

---

1. This definition includes traditional food and beverage products (except fish and fish products), and a range of other products such as raw textiles like wool and cotton, hides and skins, live animals, and some manufacturing products such as caseins that are derived from animals or plants.

Table 2 provides more information on the top 10 imports at the disaggregated HS 6 code level. During the first six months of 2007, these imports were 3.8 per cent of total Chinese imports, a figure down from the 6.6 per cent during the last six months of 1996. By value, total agricultural imports were US$ 16,459 million during the first six months of 2007, up from US$ 5,030 million in the final six months of 1996. By product, the main imports were soybeans (US and Brazil), cotton (US and India) and palm oil (Malaysia and Indonesia). Note that South Africa features as the third supplier of wool, the fourth major import. Overall, the top 10 imports make up 68.6 per cent of the total agricultural imports in the latest period.

Table 2: China's agricultural imports, 1996 and 2007 (six monthly data), US$ millions

HS	Description	Jul-Dec 1996	Jan-Jun 2007	Sources of Imports 2007		
Total Imports		75,689	434,185			
Total Agricultural Imports $m		5,030	16,459	First	Second	Third
Total Agricultural Imports %		6.6%	3.8%			
120100	Soybeans	239.1	4,533.4	US	Brazil	Argentina
520100	Cotton	436.7	1,593.8	US	India	Uzbekistan
151190	Palm Oil	179.3	1,354.9	Malaysia	Indonesia	
510111	Wool	182.0	860.6	Australia	New Zealand	RSA
150710	Soybean Oil	310.5	746.3	Argentina	Brazil	US
410150	Hides & Skins	0.0	579.0	US	Australia	EU
230120	Flour/Fish Meal	248.3	576.1	Peru	Chile	US
071410	Cassava	1.4	475.4	Thailand	Vietnam	
020714	Chicken Cuts	78.6	389.9	US	Brazil	Argentina
240120	Tobacco	8.2	183.3	Zimbabwe	US	Zambia
Subtotal above $m		1,684.1	11,292.6			
Subtotal above % agriculture		33.5%	68.6%			

Source: World Trade Atlas (2007)

2.4.2 *China's Agricultural Exports*

Figure 5 shows a similar profile for China's agricultural exports as shown in Figure 4 for agricultural imports. While the dollar figure (on the right hand axis) is steadily climbing, the percentage share of Chinese exports (on the left hand axis) is consistently downward. Thus, while agricultural exports are increasing, they are not really part of the dramatic overall Chinese export explosion of recent times.

Figure 5: China's agricultural exports as a percenage of total exports and total exports (biannual data)

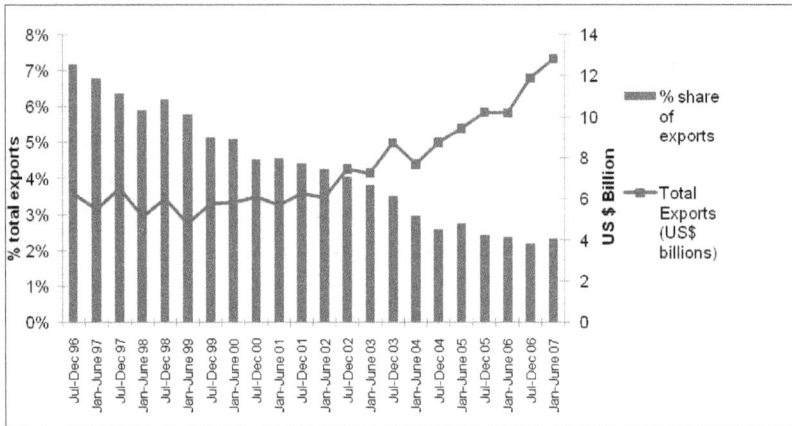

Source: World Trade Atlas (2007)

Table 3 further elaborates China's agricultural exports. The top 10 exports accounted for 28.3 per cent of the agricultural exports in the most recent six-monthly period. Maize, apple juice and garlic are the major exports, with Korea, the US and Indonesia being the main destinations. The right hand column shows the recent ranking of South Africa as a destination for China's agricultural exports. Note that on three occasions South Africa has ranked in eighth position or higher. Particularly relevant are the high position as exports enjoyed by apple juice and apples, as these are an export interest for South Africa.

Table 3: China's agricultural exports, 1996 and 2007 (six monthly data),US$ millions and destination

HS	Description	Jul-Dec 1996	Jan-Jun 2007	Destination	
Total Exports		87,017.8	546,922.8	Main	RSA
Total Agricultural Exports $b		6,256.6	12,807.0		Ranking
Total Agricultural Exports %		7.2%	2.3%		
100590	Maize	27.1	605.5	Korea	13
200979	Apple Juice	0.0	551.2	US	8
070320	Garlic	80.8	426.1	Indonesia	74
200310	Mushrooms Prep	84.6	377.5	EU	37
160232	Chicken Meat	33.2	349.7	Japan	5
071290	Vegetables Dried	122.5	328.2	Japan	14
050400	Animal Guts	183.4	266.7	EU	4
080810	Apples	37.8	244.7	Russia	N/A
210690	Food Preparations	85.3	240.6	Japan	17
200290	Tomato Paste	16.6	231.2	EU	21
Subtotal above $bn		671.4	3,621.5		
Subtotal above % agricultural		10.7%	28.3%		

Source: World Trade Atlas (2007)

2.5 South Africa's Agricultural Trade

2.5.1 South Africa's Agricultural Trade with the World

Over the period from September 1997 through to September 2007 the average growth rate in South Africa's agricultural exports was 9.2 per cent, with the top four entries of wine, citrus, grapes and apples all exceeding this growth. Sugar and prepared fruits exhibited lower rates, while maize (the main export in 1997), peanuts, wheat, jams and barley all exhibited negative growth over the period. Agricultural exports remain concentrated in a small number of tariff lines, with horticultural exports predominating, if one includes wine in a broad definition of horticulture. The EU remains the largest destination for agricultural exports but there has been a rapid increase in exports to the rest of Africa. Argentina has emerged as the main source of food and agricultural imports into South Africa (largely animal feed, a consequence of the rapid increase in poultry consumption), followed by the US, the UK, Australia and Zimbabwe.

2.5.2 South Africa's Agricultural Trade with China

During 2006, South Africa exported some US$ 69.36 million in agricultural products to China (Table 4). Almost half (US$ 31.37 million) of these exports were wool, followed by sugar and fish meal[1]. The average duty that would have been assessed on South African imports at the Chinese border would have been 13.96 per cent[2]. Conversely, South Africa imported agricultural products to the value of US$ 127.21 million, with sausage casings and kidney beans being the main imports. The assessed average duty at the South African border would have been 6.79 per cent. Agricultural exports to China represented 3.41 per cent of total South African exports to China in 2006 (up from the 2.56 per cent in 2004 but down marginally from 3.61 per cent in 2005), while the imports represented 1.87 per cent of the total imports from China (very similar to the 1.83 per cent in 2004 but up from the 1.4 per cent in 2005).

Table 4: South African agricultural trade with China, 2006

RSA exports to China	US $Million	Duty	Imports from China	US $Million	Duty
Wool	31.37	1.0	Sausage casings	25.19	0.0
Sugar	9.27	50.0	kidney beans	22.49	10.0
Fish Meal	5.04	2.0	fruit juices	7.69	0.0
Sheep Skins	4.23	7.0	Peptones	4.65	0.0
Sausage Casings	4.01	18.0	proc tomatoes	4.64	15.0
Tobacco	2.75	10.0	Herbs	3.90	2.5
Total agricultural exports from RSA to China	$69.36m	13.96%	Total agricultural imports into RSA from China	$127.21m	6.79%

Source: World Trade Atlas (2006)

1. Fish meal is arguably not an agricultural product.
2. The average duty was assessed on Chinese import data and not South African export data. These two values do not reconcile.

Exports of agricultural products represented 1.56 per cent of total Chinese exports to South Africa (down marginally from the 1.75 per cent in both 2004 and 2005), while the agricultural imports were 1.52 per cent of the imports from South Africa during 2006 (up from 0.44 per cent in 2004 and 1.01 per cent in 2005).

2.5.3 Competition Dynamics in China's Market

While South Africa is taking a closer look at the Chinese market, it is as well to remember that other nations are following suit. Particularly crucial here are fellow southern hemisphere competitors in seasonal products, competitors such as Australia, Chile, Brazil and New Zealand. This sub-section will concentrate on the example of New Zealand to see how South Africa is competing against it in the Chinese agricultural market. This comparison is relevant as (a) both South Africa and New Zealand are southern hemisphere countries producing some similar products and (b) New Zealand was the first country in the world to actually begin negotiations with China for an FTA.

During 2005, China imported agricultural goods as defined by the WTO to the value of US$ 637.7 million from New Zealand but only US$ 46.9 million from South Africa: New Zealand had a market share of 2.43 per cent compared with South Africa's much lower 0.18 per cent[1]. Both countries have increased their shares since 1995: New Zealand's from 1.96 per cent and South Africa's from 0.13 percent. In assessing overall imports into China, South Africa's market share was 0.52 per cent during 2005 (the same as for 1995) while New Zealand's share was a lesser 0.20 per cent, a decline from the 1995 market share of 0.26 percent. China is therefore more important to South Africa for non-agricultural trade in contrast to the situation in New Zealand, although both New Zealand and South Africa have increased their non-agricultural trade faster than their agricultural trade.

To further examine this trade, we narrowed the analysis down to a more manageable scope by selecting the HS 6 lines for which global imports into China were at least US$ 100,000 during 2005. This yielded 592 lines in total, but only 150 of these had combined imports from New Zealand and South Africa of at least US$ 10,000. For both New Zealand and South Africa, this accounted for 100 per cent of their agricultural imports into China. Interestingly, these same lines accounted for 97.8 per cent of the agricultural imports from New Zealand during 1995, but only 10.7 per cent of the imports during that year from South Africa. An examination of the data shows that imports of barley of US$ 11.7 million in 1995 and US$ 5.1 million in 1996 dominated agricultural imports in the early years. These imports have not been repeated since. An analysis of South Africa's major imports shows:

1) Waste products for animal feed to be the main import, followed by oranges and cane sugar;

---

1. For the six months ending 30 June 2007, New Zealand's share of agricultural imports into China had reduced marginally to 2.36 per cent while South Africa's had increased to 0.39 percent.

2) Only two products have a market share above 10 per cent (oranges and ethyl alcohol); and

3) New Zealand is a competitor in food wastes, oranges, wool, ethyl alcohol and fish oils.

In 2005, the top 10 South African imports accounted for 84.4 per cent of agricultural imports, and the top 20 accounted for a large 95.3 percent. A similar profile for New Zealand gives the respective figures of 73.7 and 88.5 per cent for the top 10 and top 20 imports by value during 2005. An analysis of the New Zealand top 10 imports shows these to be concentrated in dairy, wool and meat, and only in meat imports does South Africa offer any competition whatever for the top 10 (although waste foods and oranges are both in the New Zealand top 20).

In nine of the top 10, New Zealand holds a market share above 20 per cent, and in seven of these ten the New Zealand market share has increased since 1995. Also, in seven out of 10 cases the overall increase in these imports into China was above the Chinese average for all agricultural products, showing that New Zealand is doing very well in the product lines that it competes in. In contrast, for the South African top 10 in only two cases are imports in the overall product line increasing faster than the agricultural average, although in all cases the South African increase is greater – perhaps South Africa is doing well in the wrong products? Another indication of the relative strength of New Zealand is that in 14 individual lines South Africa has a market share above 5 per cent while New Zealand's comparable figure is 73 lines.

An interesting comparison to make between South Africa and New Zealand is to take the example of wine imports into China. In 2005, China's wine imports were worth some US$ 75 million, with the market dominated by France and Spain (a combined 46 per cent share). Trailing in tenth and eleventh places were South Africa and New Zealand respectively, with imports of US$ 0.6 million each. New Zealand's growth rate of imports since 1996 has been the fastest of any of the majors, while South Africa's has been just above the overall average. Since 1997, the average values of imports per litre from the different sources has been relatively consistent, and the highest average value has been New Zealand, at 4.0 times the overall average. South Africa's average price consistently averages around half the comparable New Zealand figure. These figures are confirmed by examining wine imports into the UK, the major market for both New Zealand and South Africa, and the US market. Thus, New Zealand is consistently outperforming South Africa in the price stakes – better wine or better marketing?

Other than wine, there are few products where New Zealand and South Africa compete head-to-head in the Chinese market. Both are significant suppliers of wastes for animal feeds and wool. The former cannot really be considered a differentiated product, while the latter also has many characteristics of a traded commodity and is thus not a good candidate for performance comparisons.

In looking to the future and visualising an FTA between China and SACU/ South Africa, there appear to be some sectors where South Africa may gain. These are limited to possibly wool, meat and some other crops, certainly sugar and processed fruits that contain sugar, and possibly some other relatively minor sectors. However, these gains are not likely to be major. Conversely, New Zealand's agricultural sector can expect to gain from an FTA with China: for example, dairy exports to China will increase substantially, and this is important as dairy exports to China are already considerable (dairy products were the single largest agricultural commodity New Zealand exported to China during 2005 at 18 per cent of the total).

2.5.4 *Factors Limiting South Africa's Exports to China*

2.5.4.1 'Trade-Chilling' Effects of Tariffs

Both quantitative and qualitative analyses and projections of the welfare effects of tariff liberalisation traditionally focus on current trade flows. Such approaches are unable to reveal new opportunities. It is conceivable, for instance, for South Africa to have relatively concentrated trade flows in specific product categories, one reason for this being that the tariff structure outside those product lines is relatively high. In short, as a consequence of these tariffs, trade may have been 'chilled'[1].

In order to establish whether South African agricultural trade into the Chinese market has been 'chilled' for some reason, it is necessary to identify where there is evidence of South African export activity. We have analysed South African global trade and compared it with the trade into China. If, as a result of this analysis and comparison, it is found that a global trade exists in a particular product line, but that the trade in the same line with China is limited or non-existent and that China does import from others, then one may possibly argue there is (a) evidence of a chilling effect and (b) potential for more trade with that country. A more elegant way to undertake this analysis is to benchmark exports to China against exports to a similar country, for example, the duty-free destination of Hong Kong. We eschewed this option, as Hong Kong and China have such a close trading relationship that this comparison would become meaningless. There really is no similar country to China in world trade!

Recognising that this analysis is rather open-ended, we have concentrated on 2005 trade data, but have occasionally adopted an historical perspective. Analysis was undertaken on a combination of the HS 4 tariff lines (and not the more detailed HS 6 lines used until now) where global imports into China were at least US$ 1 million during 2005 to represent the demand side, and these were then compared with the respective HS 4 tariff lines exported to global markets from South Africa during 2005 to represent the supply side. From there, six categories were examined. These categories are:

---

1. Note also that, in effect, a trade reconciliation exercise is conducted in this section to compare the Chinese import data used above with South African export data.

1) Where South African imports had at least a 1 per cent market share in China;
2) Where at least 1 per cent of South African exports went to China;
3) Where South Africa records positive exports to China in 2005 but China does not record positive imports from South Africa;
4) Where positive imports into China from South Africa are recorded but no exports from South Africa are reported;
5) Where there is at least US$ 5 million exported from South Africa globally but no reported imports of this trade reported into China from South Africa; and
6) As in (5) above, but where South Africa reports less than US$ 5 million in global exports (but above US$ 500,000).

The key points from this trade-chilling analysis (by category as above) are:
1) South Africa has at least a 1 per cent market share in the following imports to China: citrus fruits, sugar, ethyl alcohol, plants, processed fruits and nuts, wool, live animals and fats and oils. There are nine HS 4 lines, and these imports accounted for 49.5 per cent of the total imports from South Africa into China during 2005. The overall average market share into China was 4.2 per cent.
2) At least 1 per cent of South Africa's exports to China include main products that do not feature in category 1 above (i.e., do not feature as much in Chinese imports as they do in South African exports). These are animal by-products (US$ 2.5 million), hides and skins (US$ 7.5 million) and cotton (US$ 8.6 million). This category accounted for 62.3 per cent of agricultural exports from South Africa to China.
3) Positive exports from South Africa that may or may not be reported as imports comprise a small mix of products in which South Africa could possibly be doing better. Lines of interest concentrate on hides and skins, and overall this group is 7.2 per cent of South Africa's exports to China.
4) Chinese imports from South Africa that were recorded in the Chinese data but not reported in South Africa as exports include very low values of Chinese imports and they represent only 0.7 per cent of the total. There are some lines in which South African global exports are significant, such as corn (maize), [?] nuts and water, but for these products there may be good reason why they are not traded with China.
5) This category, potentially the most important for examination, focuses on goods South Africa exported worth at least US$ 5 million globally in 2005, which are imported by China from global markets but not from South Africa. As such, the twain did not meet. This clearly shows there are both supply and demand factors that are not, for whatever reason, meeting. By value, the main agricultural export items from South Africa include apples, apricots, pineapples and avocados, the recurring hides and skins, chocolate products and processed foods (including processed meats).

6) As in 5 above, but this time South African exports globally were less than US$ 5 million, making these products a lesser priority if we assume that exports are facing supply constraints in South Africa. This is effectively an empty set for agricultural products.

2.5.4.2 'Trade-Chilling' Effects of China's Sensitive Sectors and Tariff Rate Quotas

At present, China administers Tariff Rate Quotas[1] (TRQs) on the following agricultural products: wheat, corn, rice, edible vegetable oil (bean oil, palm oil and rape seed oil), sugar, wool, wool tops and cotton. Analysis of the trade data shows that there are some TRQ products interspersed among the six categories above. As these sectors represent sensitive sectors into China, it is important to consider current and potential access for South Africa in these products.

A point to make is that there are products of interest to South Africa in this list. In particular, these are wool and sugar, but potentially wheat, maize, rice, soya bean oil and cotton, which have all been exported from South Africa globally in the last four calendar years. These TRQ products therefore represent potential opportunities for South African trade negotiators to concentrate on, with sugar probably the priority. Here the in-quota tariff is 15 per cent, while the out-of-quota rate is an almost prohibitive 50 per cent. In earlier analyses of agricultural products, the Trade Law Centre for Southern Africa (tralac) found that, except for sugar, the tariffs may not necessarily be the limiting constraint into the Chinese market for South Africa.

---

1. Further discussion on China's non-tariff barriers (NTBs) and TRQs is presented in section 4.

3. Modelling the Possible Role of Chinese Imports in Stimulating Future South African Exports

Regional trade agreements (RTAs) are becoming increasingly popular as a trade policy tool, and SACU/South Africa is embracing this concept with a view to furthering bilateral trade. Pending the resolution of a few outstanding issues, the preferential trade deal with the Mercado Común del Sur (MERCOSUR)[1] seems to be on track. Also, an FTA between SACU and European Free Trade Area[2] has virtually been concluded, after a long delay. SACU members are in serious discussion with the European Union about EPAs and an extension of the TDCA. A trade deal with India has been mooted and SACU is considering talks with China.

In this section, we explore the implications of a South African/China trade agreement as part of which all tariffs are reduced to zero using the Global Trade Analysis Project (GTAP) model. The model assesses the full implications of such an FTA agreement against what the likely agricultural trade would be in the absence of such an agreement. We start by discussing the widely used broad-based GTAP computer model and presenting results of tralac simulations using this model. After noting some of the limitations of this broad GTAP approach, we then focus the study on two South African agricultural-specific computer models to link the GTAP results to a more detailed level.

3.1. The GTAP Model[3]

GTAP is supported by a fully documented, publicly available global database and the underlying software for data manipulation and implementing the model. The framework is a system of multisector, country economy-wide models linked at the sector level through trade flows between commodities and factors of production. The 2007 GTAP database (version 6) divides the global economy into 96 regions, with 57 sectors of economic activity in each region, and work is constantly under way to expand this country/regional and commodity coverage. We note that for SACU these regional aggregations are South Africa, Botswana and an amalgamation of Lesotho, Namibia and Swaziland into one 'rest of SACU country'. This latter is a severe limitation for examining the regional impact in detail, as of course Lesotho, Namibia and Swaziland have three entirely different economies.

GTAP is a comparatively static, general equilibrium model, which means that while it examines all aspects of an economy through its general equilibrium feature

---

1. MERCOSUR member countries are Brazil, Argentina, Uruguay and Paraguay.
2. EFTA member states include Switzerland, Norway, Iceland and Liechtenstein.
3. GTAP is a global network of researchers who conduct quantitative analyses of international economic policy issues, especially trade policy, using at least some variant of a standard GTAP model. They cooperate to produce a consistent global economic database, covering many sectors and all parts of the world. This database contains bilateral trade patterns, production, consumption and intermediate use of commodities and services data. See the website at www.gtap.agecon.purdue.

(as distinct from a partial equilibrium approach that examines only the sector under consideration), it is static in the sense that it does not specifically incorporate dynamics such as improved technology and economies of scale unless these are specifically built in. The economic agents of consumers, producers and government are modelled according to neoclassical economic theory, with producers maximising returns to factor income and consumers maximising their utility, markets perfectly competitive, and all regions and activities linked. Thus, a small change in, say, a tariff into South Africa will have repercussions right through the world, but of course in practice those repercussions can be largely ignored in almost all of the full model and limited to key actors only. Results are measured as a change in welfare arising principally from the reallocation of resources within an economy and the resulting change in allocative efficiency and terms of trade effects[1], which may be significant in many instances. This welfare is based upon a representative household, so unless this aspect is modified it is not possible to examine the distributional aspects other than through the skilled/unskilled labour market closures. The standard GTAP model also does not address the time-path of benefits and capital flows over time. These changes are important as they allow consumers to borrow, which in turn allows consumption patterns to vary over time.

The analysis here is based on a variant of the GTAP model described in Sandrey and Jensen (2007) to assess the impact of possible multilateral market access reforms resulting from an FTA between South Africa (technically SACU but predominantly South Africa) and China. The FTA primary scenario considered in this simulation entails the results of the removal of trade barriers between China and the SACU member countries (predominantly South Africa) as measured in 2015 in a world shaped by the baseline scenario. This implies that all ad valorem tariffs and ad valorem equivalents of specific tariffs between China and all the SACU countries are abolished. Differences between the so-called baseline scenario and this so-called primary scenario are therefore the results of the implementation of the SACU/China FTA.

3.2 Findings from a GTAP Simulation of a SACU-China Free Trade Agreement

The overall results can be summed up as follows:

1) The welfare results for South Africa are US$ 277 million.
2) The gains by China are US$ 314 million.
3) South African exports to China are US$ 579 million, and the increased South African imports from China are US$ 1,546 million.

---

1. Where terms of trade are the relative changes in import and export prices following a change. Indeed, it is generally improved allocative efficiency within a country as it moves resources into more internationally competitive activities that leads to the outcome of greater welfare following a reduction in border protection. Thus, often the allocative efficiency pathway is providing most of the benefits to the 'home' country from reducing its own protection in a bilateral FTA rather than the exporter gaining better market access into foreign markets. This is an example of where a general equilibrium model is often able to counter the common mercantilist argument that a country needs protection to develop its own industrial sector.

3.2.1 Projected Changes in Trade Flows

Table 5 lists the aggregate overall changes to trade flows for the partner countries in 2015, expressed as percentage changes for both exports and imports and then in US$ million for the trade balance. South Africa has marginally increased exports globally once all markets are accounted for, as does China with a higher dollar value.

Table 5: Percentage change in the quantity of total imports/exports and trade balance, 2015

	South Africa	Botswana	SACU	China
Exports %	1.1	0.3	1.1	0.1
Imports %	1.5	0.3	0.9	0.1
Trade Balance US$ Million	0	0	-2	118

Source: GTAP results

The change in the free on board (fob) export prices of commodities facing South Africa's producers varied between -1.76 per cent for wearing apparel and 1.23 per cent for other manufactures. The change in the (cif) import prices of commodities facing South Africa's importers varied between -0.06 per cent for textiles and 0.28 per cent for fish. Of interest from an agricultural perspective is the increase in the export price of sugar (0.66 per cent), other horticulture crops (1.19 per cent), wool (0.88 per cent) and vegetables and fruit (0.09 per cent).

Other results show that in the agricultural sector South Africa increases exports to China by US$ 103 million, and importantly, there is only trade diversion from other destinations of some US$ 30 million. Thus, some US$ 73 million of this agricultural trade is new trade. Of the total increase, most is in other crops (US$ 20 million) and sugar (US$ 23 million), while there are small global reductions in vegetables and fruit in particular. For imports, there is a marginal increase in South African imports from China of US$ 14 million (US$ 6 million in beverages and tobacco) that leads to the overall change in agricultural imports of US$ 17 million. In summary, there is little action in the agricultural sectors following an FTA between China and South Africa (SACU).

3.2.2 Projected Welfare Impact

Results from the GTAP simulation show the changes in welfare from the FTA assuming a complete 100 per cent reduction in merchandise tariffs, with the data expressed in US$ million as one-off increases in annual welfare at the assessed end point of 2015. South Africa's gains amount to US$ 277 million, a figure similar to but lower than China's US$ 314 million. In further examining the GTAP results, the following was found:

1) South Africa's welfare gains are split between gains from better access into China of US$ 205 million and US$ 105 million through reductions in its own tariffs,

but there are reductions of US$ 33 million in South Africa's welfare as China gains better access into the BLNS (Botswana, Lesotho, Namibia and Swaziland) countries.

2) China's gains are dominated by gains of US$ 260 million from increased access into South Africa and US$ 34 million from the better access into BLNS.

3.3 Limitations of the GTAP Model

One technical problem for models and modellers is the aggregation problem. The latest GTAP version contains data on and linkages between 57 sectors (42 for the production of goods and the remaining 15 for service sectors) and the option of 96 country/regional possibilities. While this sounds impressive, it is not really adequate for anything other than indicative results at an aggregated level.

For example, nestled in the productive sectors there are two of relevance to the fruit sector: (a) vegetables, fruit and nuts, and (b) food products not elsewhere classified. The former represents largely primary unprocessed products, while the latter is processed products. We are, literally, mixing fresh apples and processed apples here, thus an important change in the market access conditions for, say, fresh apples may often make a miniscule change to the overall picture that cannot be identified by a GTAP analysis. This is not to decry or degrade the use of a GTAP model: rather, it is to point out that such an aggregate model loses its richness when detail is important. This is why we explore the use of more disaggregated models in the next section, in order to link the 'big picture' GTAP results to the very disaggregated BFAP and PROVIDE models.

3.4 Findings from Extended Econometric Analysis[1]

Different trade models have been used in South Africa to examine the impacts of trade liberalisation on production and welfare in the economy. These different models focus on different aspects of the problem, from global models that look at the 'big picture' through to sector models that examine the industries and the welfare results in more detail. The objective of this brief section is to introduce the linking of these models from the GTAP model to the more agricultural-specific models.

The first example looks at importing apples from China into South Africa, and here the Chinese imports are proxied by modelling the importation of 10,000 tonnes of apples annually (Reynolds, 2007). As shown earlier, apples (and apple juice) are a major export from China, so this is an entirely feasible scenario. This is done by using the price impacts from the GTAP model, with these introduced into the Bureau of Food and Agricultural Policy (BFAP) sector model in order to simulate industry impacts.

---

1. This section is largely reproduced from Ferdinand Meyer, Cecilia Punt, Sanri Reynolds and Ron Sandrey, 2008. "Modelling the South African-China trading relationship", tralac Trade brief 2, January 2008. Note that the terms 'South Africa' and 'SACU' are used at different times.

The second example examines the implications of a SACU-China FTA on South Africa by using the PROVIDE model, with the objective of looking at the distributional implications and welfare effects of an FTA specifically for the South African economy. This model is useful for estimating the welfare and distributional implications of an FTA for the South African economy, while at the same time highlighting the implications for the agricultural sector at a provincial level

3.4.1 The BFAP Model

Only the sugar and apple industry impacts are included in this section, which presents an attempt to combine the technical results of a possible FTA between SACU and China from three distinct modelling approaches. The methodology followed to ensure the compatibility of the modelling outputs is not presented in this brief. The outcomes of the models are discussed and the main findings summarised. Important to note is the fact that the analysis does not take any non-tariff barrier reductions into account.

From the changes in import and export prices between different regions of the world that were simulated by the GTAP model, the changes in the weighted average import and export prices faced by South African producers and the Rest of the World could be determined in order to shock the PROVIDE and BFAP models. Of interest from an agricultural perspective is the increase in the export price of sugar (+0.66 per cent), other horticulture crops (+1.19 per cent), wool (+0.88 per cent) and vegetables and fruit (0.09 per cent) under the FTA scenario.

Production decisions are influenced by changes in relative prices fetched on the domestic and export markets. Total production, which comprises production for the domestic market and the export market, reflects the expansion or contraction of the different industries. The biggest decrease in volume of production is for electronic equipment (-0.54 per cent) while the biggest increase is for other manufactures (0.96 per cent). The model suggests that the production of grains increases (-0.05 per cent) but the production of oil seeds (-0.06 per cent) decreases. However, there is an increase in the production of sugar cane, which supports the increase in the production of sugar. The BFAP sector model was shocked with the increase in the export price of sugar (from GTAP model).

Table 6 presents the impacts on the sugar market over the period 2011-15, as simulated in the BFAP sector model. An increase (0.22 per cent on average) in the recoverable value of sugar cane induces an expansion in the area under sugar cane of only 0.05 per cent on average. This clearly points to the inelastic nature of sugar cane production. Interestingly, there is no shift in the domestic use of sugar and the increase in sugar production is completely absorbed by the export market. This can be explained by the fact that the domestic sugar price is a regulated price that is not directly affected by the export price of sugar or the domestic sugar cane price. Sugar exports increase by more than 0.10 per cent.

Table 6: BFAP results – Percentage change in the SA sugar market

	2011	2012	2013	2014	2015
Area under sugar cane	0.03%	0.04%	0.04%	0.05%	0.05%
Sugar cane average yield	0.00%	0.00%	0.00%	0.00%	0.00%
Sugar cane production	0.02%	0.03%	0.04%	0.05%	0.05%
Sugar cane for sugar	0.02%	0.03%	0.04%	0.05%	0.05%
Sugarcane for ethanol	0.00%	0.00%	0.00%	0.00%	0.00%
Sugar domestic use	0.00%	0.00%	0.00%	0.00%	0.00%
Sugar exports	0.05%	0.07%	0.09%	0.11%	0.12%
Sugar recoverable value	0.21%	0.22%	0.22%	0.23%	0.23%
Sugar cane average price	0.21%	0.21%	0.22%	0.22%	0.22%

Source: BFAP model (2007)

The export price of vegetables and fruits increases by 0.09 per cent (from the GTAP model). The GTAP model makes no clear distinction between the various categories of vegetables and fruits and therefore the BFAP sector model could not be shocked with the shift in the export price. Yet, some of the industries that fall into this category could be very sensitive to an FTA of this nature, especially since China is a low-cost producer and local industries could struggle to compete against cheaper imports. The apple industry is a good example. An independent assumption was made to shock the BFAP apple sector model. It was assumed that 10,000 tons of apples would be imported from China annually over the period 2008–12.

The results show that in 2008 the volume of apples sold in the domestic market increases by 3 per cent and the local price decreases by 4.2 per cent due to the increased level of imports. The 4.2 per cent decline is equivalent to R149/ton (nominal terms). Due to the lower domestic price, more apples will initially be exported (exports increase by 1 per cent) and less of the domestic crop will be allocated to the local market. The lower domestic prices lead to lower production and export levels in the long run. However, local production will decline over time as a consequence of lower domestic prices and therefore exports will also decline over the long run.

3.4.2 The PROVIDE Model

This section uses the research from Punt (2007) that analyses the potential socioeconomic implications of the FTA for South Africa using a single country computable general equilibrium (CGE) model for South Africa called the PROVIDE model (PROVIDE, 2005). Punt's study builds on an analysis of the potential implications of a SACU-China FTA using a global (multi-regional) CGE GTAP model as discussed above.

The GTAP model indicates, among other things, the expected changes in trade levels and import and export prices faced by different regions of the world, while PROVIDE is a model specifically designed to look at South Africa in detail. The

Figure 6: BFAP results – Percentage change in the SA apple industry

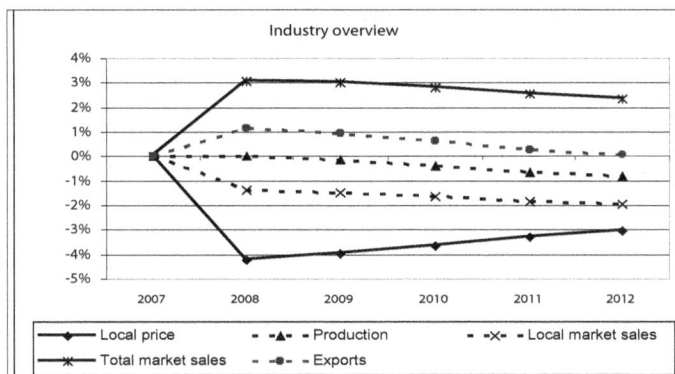

Source: BFAP model (2007)

'big picture' results from the GTAP model were [?] used in the PROVIDE model, with the objective of estimating the welfare and distributional implications of an FTA for South Africa's economy, while at the same time highlighting the implications for the agricultural sector at a provincial level.

The PROVIDE model allows for this focus because of the level of detail in the underlying social accounting matrix (SAM) from which the model is calibrated. The SAM used for this study includes 41 commodities (14 are for agriculture), 36 activities (9 are for agriculture), 41 factors and 32 households. Agricultural activities, labour and household categories are distinguished by province. Results from the GTAP model reflect a scenario of complete removal of import tariffs in both SACU and China. From the changes in import and export prices between different regions of the world, the changes in the weighted average import and export prices faced by South African producers and the 'rest of the world' could be determined. These two price vectors were used as a shock in the PROVIDE model. An attempt was made to match the commodity accounts in the SAM for South Africa as closely as possible to the production accounts in the GTAP database used for the purposes of the study.

Shifting the focus from a national to a provincial level, the PROVIDE model reports agricultural activities on aggregate per province. The weighted average changes in import and export prices for all commodities faced by South African industries and markets generated with the GTAP model were introduced as a single shock to the PROVIDE model. Results indicate an increase in agricultural production in Gauteng province (+0.21 per cent), followed by Eastern Cape (+0.12 per cent), KwaZulu-Natal (+0.07 per cent) and Mpumalanga (0.03 per cent). The net impact on production in the Western Cape is negligible, while North-West (-0.07 per cent), Northern Cape (-0.05 per cent), Limpopo (-0.03 per cent) and Free State (-0.02 per cent) experience a decline in production on aggregate. The results are driven by the combinations of products produced within each of the provinces.

31

The change in economic activity (not only in agriculture but for the complete economy) impacts on factor demands and wage rates. When the full employment assumption is relaxed for unskilled workers, aggregate labour income increases by 0.066 per cent and 3,575 employment opportunities are created throughout the economy, of which 1,144 (32 per cent) are created in Gauteng, followed by North-West (697 or 19 per cent).

Table 7: CGE results – Employment creation

	Number	Share
Gauteng	1,144	32%
North-West	697	19%
Free State	511	14%
KwaZulu-Natal	373	10%
Eastern Cape	323	9%
Limpopo	247	7%
Western Cape	156	4%
Northern Cape	97	3%
Mpumalanga	28	1%
Total	3,575	100%

Source: PROVIDE MODEL (2007)

The macroeconomic results from the PROVIDE model indicated an increase of 0.02 per cent in the gross domestic product of South Africa from the given changes in world prices faced by South Africa's producers and consumers as derived from the GTAP model results. The exchange rate appreciates by 0.02 per cent. However, if the exchange rate is fixed and the external balance is free to adjust, then the trade balance improves by R 3.85 billion.

However, the most notable changes in the agricultural sector are the increases in the production of wool (0.3 per cent) and other horticultural crops (0.59 per cent), mainly in response to higher prices in the international market. The production results can also be analysed from an activity (as opposed to a product) point of view. Agricultural activities are reported on aggregate per province. Results indicate an increase in agricultural production in Gauteng (0.21 per cent), followed by Eastern Cape (0.12 per cent), KwaZulu-Natal (0.07 per cent) and Mpumalanga (0.03 per cent). The model suggests that the provinces of the North-West (-0.07 per cent), Northern Cape (-0.05 per cent), Limpopo (-0.03 per cent) and Free State (-0.02 per cent) experience declines in production on aggregate. The net impact on production in the Western Cape is negligible. The results are driven by the combinations of products produced in each of the provinces.

The change in economic activity impacts on factor demands and wage rates. Aggregate labour income increases by 0.059 per cent when full employment in the economy is assumed. In this scenario there is no employment creation, only diversion, and the increase in income is mainly driven by a net increase in wage rates. The increases in factor income by labour groups in the Free State range between 0.06 per cent for highly skilled non-white labour and 0.24 per cent for semi-skilled non-white labour. In the Western Cape, the range of change is much smaller. When the full employment assumption is relaxed for unskilled workers, aggregate labour income increases by 0.066 per cent and 3,575 employment opportunities are created economy-wide, of which 1,144 (32 per cent) are created in Gauteng, followed by North-West with 697 (19 per cent).

The small but positive impact of the FTA is also reflected in the increase in welfare of R 313 million (2000 values). This welfare measure only takes into account changes in household income and changes in consumer prices and can be seen as a type of measure to reflect changes in the purchasing power of different households: as such it is not directly comparable to the welfare measure produced by the GTAP model. The consumer price changes range between -0.31 per cent for other manufactures and +0.12 per cent for fish.

3.5 Concluding Comments

This section provides an introduction to the arcane world of trade modelling. In particular, it explores the potential gains from an FTA between China and South Africa with a particular focus on the agricultural sector. Starting from the 'big picture' GTAP global model, it finds that there are useful gains from such an FTA for South Africa. However, few of these gains are found in the agricultural sector – as could be expected after exploring the agricultural trading relationship between the two partners in the first section of this paper. Furthermore, the GTAP results are too aggregated to give much insight into the precise sectoral, regional and household categories in South Africa.

Turning to firstly the BFAP model and then the PROVIDE model, we are able to focus on some more details for the apple and sugar sectors using BFAP and then the provincial income distributional effects. This was undertaken in order to demonstrate how these models can be linked to maximise the policy advice that can be gleaned from modelling exercises.

4. Non-tariff Barriers (NTBs)

4.1 An overview of NTBs

Prior to its accession to the WTO in 2001, China restricted imports through high tariffs, discriminatory taxes, import quotas, restrictions on trading rights and other NTBs. Thus, the WTO accession agreement required the country to phase out its import quota system, apply international norms to its testing and standards administration, remove local content requirements and make its import licensing and registration schemes transparent.

However, while over the past two decades China's average tariff on imported products, including agriculture, has declined (for instance, from 45 per cent in 1992 to 15 per cent by 2005) following the acceptance of the WTO accession protocol, this reduction of tariffs has now shifted the market access focus more to the role of non-tariff barriers in impeding trade flows[1].

While China has made some progress in addressing its NTBs, such as revising local content regulations and removing import quotas, Donnelly and Manifold (2005) report that many industries face increasing NTBs. Such barriers include regulations that set high thresholds for entry into service sectors such as banking and insurance, selective and unwarranted inspection requirements for agricultural products, and the use of questionable SPS measures and manipulation of technical standards to limit imports.

Nevertheless, estimating what benefit could arise from China's liberalisation of its NTBs first requires knowing the *ad valorem* equivalence of those barriers (that is, the NTBs need to be approximated by a tariff equivalent). Approximating the tariff equivalence of NTBs is a difficult exercise, with the required data being rarely available. Necessary for this approximation is the landed price of an imported product and the ex-factory price for a comparable domestic product. Alternatively, if comparable products cannot be found, then the price of the same product exported to China and to another 'benchmark' region that is unprotected (such as Hong Kong) can be used. The price differential between the imported and local product (or between the same product exported to two different markets) once tariffs, transportation costs and any other non-discriminatory taxes are taken into account, can be attributed to NTBs.

4.2 Assessment of NTBs

The working definition of non-tariff barriers (NTBs) used in this paper is *"government measures other than tariffs that unnecessarily restrict trade flows"*. This covers a range of measures from health and safety measures through to the suite of regulations associated with trade and general matters such as transport costs, and customs and administration procedures that may not be directly under the control of gov

---

1. See OECD (2005).

ernments but are certainly under its influence. In this section, three broad groups (admittedly sometimes arbitrary) are supplied to assist in understanding these regulatory instruments.

The first grouping is those measures that are put in place to protect the health and safety of both consumers and the environment in importing countries. These measures can be and often are viewed as inhibiting trade when viewed from the exporter's perspective. This category is

a) *health, safety and environment* measures including import and export bans, SPS requirements and standards and conformance requirements.

The second group comprises a wide range of regulations that are in place for a variety of reasons. This category is

b) *trade policy regulations.* These are broader policy measures, including export assistance, export taxes, import licences, import quotas, production subsidies, state trading and import monopolies, tax concessions, trade remedies practices (i.e., anti dumping, safeguard and countervailing duty measures). Issues such as tariff escalation and issues associated with regional trading arrangements themselves also fall into this category.

The third category is not generally regulation *per se*, but rather a wide grouping of procedures and factors that operate in a manner that generally inhibits trade flows. This category is

c) *administrative disincentives to export:* customs clearance delays, lack of transparency and consistency in customs procedures, overly bureaucratic (and often arbitrary) processing and documentation requirements for consignments, high freight transport charges and services that are not user-friendly.

It is important to note that many NTBs that are viewed by exporters as 'trade restricting' are legitimate requirements (such as health, safety and environmental measures from a) above and costs of doing business that are included in c) above). These measures become NTBs when they are applied in a discriminatory manner or when they become overly bureaucratic and the costs associated with them excessive.

4.3 Specific NTBs against Agricultural Exports to China and their Impact

Table 8 presents an overview of the main NTBs against agricultural exports to China as reported by Donnelly and Manifold (2005).

A good source of the most significant non-tariff measures impacting China's agricultural imports is the report *Agriculture in China: Development and significance for Australia* (ABARE, 2006:45-58). The main NTBs discussed in the above-named report are outlined in the following sub-sections.

Table 8: Main non-tariff barriers restricting agricultural exports to China

	Plant & plant products	Food & food products	Animals and animal products	Agricultural production	Beverages (alcoholic)
Import Licensing	Cotton	Livestock (meat); Grains and nuts; Vegetable oil; Soybean oil			
Sanitary and phytosanitary measures		Fruit (Apples, Grapes, Peaches, Pears, Barley); Grains & nuts (Barley, Wheat); Meat; Vegetables (Avocados, Potatoes)	Poultry		
Standards, Testing, Certification and Labelling		Processed; Biotechnology products; Grain & nuts (Corn); Vegetables (Soybeans)			
State Trading Enterprises	Cotton	Grains & nuts; Vegetable oil		Fertilizers	
Taxes					Wine

Source: Donnelly and Manifold (2005)

4.3.1 Tariff Rate Quotas (TRQs)

The tariff quota system – implemented not only in China but also among other trading nations – is a WTO-sanctioned measure that impedes trade through a tariff that varies with specific quantities. This TRQ system is especially for agricultural products and it acts as a non-tariff barrier where the tariff applied on a product is higher once a specified quota threshold is breached[1]. The actual non-tariff barrier is thus the differentiation of tariffs in relation to quantity, but more so the strenuous administrative processes that follow, affecting timing and the extent of the quota imports to China.

The quota process, which is managed by China's Ministry of Commerce (MOFCOM)[2] and National Development and Reform Commission (NDRC)[3], was regulated in September 2003 to enhance transparency, especially regarding the allocation of these quotas. As mentioned previously, TRQs are administered on six agricultural product categories in China. These include products such as wool and sugar, but also wheat, maize, rice, etc., for which South Africa may potentially have export opportunities into China.

Other than the out-of-quota tariff, tedious administrative measures also pose barriers to trade, especially in agricultural products. This is so because the quota allocation process, controlled by the above-mentioned organisations, is subject to a

---

1. TRQs were expanded from grain and oilseed commodities when China entered the WTO, to include wheat, rice, corn, sugar, cotton, wool and some vegetable oils (OECD, 2005).
2. Responsible for the management of grain and cotton tariff quotas.
3. Responsible for the management of vegetable oils and sugar.

number of criteria that firms must meet. Tariff quotas remain great barriers to entry especially for wheat and sugar.

4.3.2 State Trading Enterprises

State Trading Enterprises (STEs), which are most notably active in grain trading, restrict the imports of certain agricultural goods into China. This is the case because these enterprises hold the exclusive rights to import particular goods, and domestic firms need to enter into import contracts through such state trading enterprises. In the agricultural sector, China National Cereals, Oils and Foodstuffs Import and Export Corporation (COFCO) is the main state trading enterprise and serves as an agent for State-Owned Enterprises (SOEs) in the domestic market. Between 1992 and 1997, more than 16 million tons of wheat, rice and maize were managed by China's state trading enterprises annually.

STEs can obtain imports at world prices and exclusively control the domestic Chinese import market. They can thus have a monopoly position as the prices at which the products are resold domestically are higher than world prices. This mark-up is partially determined by the price elasticity of demand by local consumers. On the world market, STEs also have the ability to exert monopolistic power when purchasing commodities. A restriction on imports by STEs, which decreases import demand, could reduce prices on the global market for imports.

While state trading companies still dominate the agro-food trade, government influence through the state trading system has become less direct since China's accession to the WTO.

4.3.3 Sanitary and Phytosanitary Measures

In the 1990s, China established a system of quality assurance for agricultural products that enter the country, in response to food safety concerns among domestic consumers. As part of the WTO's SPS Agreement, China sets technical standards (inspection, quarantine, etc.) on imported agricultural products for SPS reasons. Such protocols, even though they should not be trade discriminating, can act as NTBs when, under these SPS measures, products do not meet certain conditions. However, Chinese regulations with regard to scientific assessment and safety certificates for biotechnology products have been questioned, and at times it has also been reported that Chinese SPS and TBT (Technical Barriers to Trade) measures have not complied with those under the WTO. The main import that has been affected in the agricultural sector by SPS measures is soybeans.

Recently, attempts have been made to improve SPS measures in China.[1] However, discrepancies between central and provincial agencies on import requirements

---

1. This was attempted through the merger of the Domestic Standards and Conformity Assessment Agency and the China Inspection and Quarantine Agency. The merger created the Administration and Quality Supervision, Inspection and Quarantine entity and furthermore two quasigovernmental testing organisations were established (ABARE, 2006).

persist. These constitute administrative hold-ups, mainly as a result of the lack of technical capacity and drawbacks in standardising testing facilities. A major concern with regard to the implementation of China's import inspection protocols is the lack of consistency with international standards, especially the employment of different standards for different countries, and varying standards for domestic goods in comparison to foreign goods. The general lack of transparency in these measures and the dearth of advanced testing facilities also contribute to the concerns associated with Chinese SPS measures.

The importation of food products is especially costly as the application period for the import licence necessary for such products can take between two weeks and three months. Nevertheless, there are alternative options for importers such as using the services of a foreign trade operator to facilitate the customs and quarantine processes for goods. Yet this comes at an additional cost for exporters and also represents suboptimal distributional channels. Another impediment for food exporters is the new Food Hygiene Law on imported foodstuffs, which sets further standards to restrict the entry of sub-standard products into China.

4.3.4 Value-Added Tax (VAT)

All importers of goods into China must pay VAT. The normal VAT rate is 17 per cent, except for certain goods (e.g., cereal and edible vegetable oils in agricultural products, whose import is subject to a 13 per cent rate). In addition, importers of certain selected consumer goods (including tobacco, liquor) must pay consumption tax. The consumption tax rate varies from 5 per cent to 40 per cent[1].

VAT is the PRC government's top source of tax revenue. In 2002 48 per cent of total central government revenue came from VAT. This decreased to just over 34 per cent in 2004 as reported by the Ministry of Finance[2].

Rather than being neutral and equitable, VAT has acted as a non-tariff barrier for Chinese agricultural imports, as its application to domestic producers is not identical to that on imported goods, with administrative complexity clouding the process. Domestically, smaller taxpayers or wholesalers are awarded different VAT rates for their produce, and generally VAT can range between 13 and 17 per cent, with rates climbing as product refinement increases. Smaller enterprises can be levied as little as 4–6 per cent on total sales volumes.

Even when the same VAT rate may apply to both domestic and imported goods, calculations differ, with a protective bias for domestic producers[3]. VAT charged on imports is levied on the total price including cost, insurance and freight, import duties, domestic taxes. But export VAT rebates and special economic zones complicate

---

1. China-Britain Business Council, http://www.cbbc.org/market_intelligence/import_export/exporting.html
2. See http://www.mof.gov.cn/english/english.htm
3. See Box 2.4 (OECD, 2005: 116) for how VAT assessment on imported agricultural goods differs to domestic produce.

the comparison further between VAT levied on imports and on domestic products. Some VAT exemptions have also been applied to imports, which have included grains, breeding animals, cotton and fertilisers and pesticides.

5. Identifying NTBs on Western Cape Fruit Producers to China: A Survey

5.1 Methodology and Instrumentation

As part of the study, in August 2007 the Centre for Chinese Studies (CCS) in collaboration with tralac compiled a survey for agricultural producers in the Western Cape, South Africa. The survey instruments included a questionnaire to extract data to identify which barriers hamper fruit and vegetable producers in South Africa's Western Cape province in exporting to the Chinese market. Emphasis was placed on non-tariff measures. More than 80 surveys were circulated electronically to fruit, vegetable and wine producers across the province. The survey is attached in Annex B.

5.2 Overview of NTBs against Western Cape Exports of Fruits to China and their Impact

The response rate to the field survey on NTBs was small. Only 10 questionnaires were returned, of which 6 were completed and 4 partly completed[1]. The lower than expected response rate can be explained by the fact that most producers of fruit, vegetable and wine products in the Western Cape do not export their products directly to third markets, but channel them through larger exporting firms that are only responsible for exporting the product, rather than producing them.

China is not among the main destinations for Western Cape fruit and vegetable produce. Markets such as the EU are favoured under the SA-EU TDCA agreement. Respondents agreed that although South Africa's agricultural exports do not have a significant footprint in the Chinese market, China is a potential future market and business partner. Of all the survey participants, only one respondent was not currently exporting to China or not currently formulating a China strategy.

Overall, the general lack of support from the South African government with regard to exporting to China was of concern. Also, government support in the form of agricultural subsidies provided in other countries competing with South Africa in the Chinese market was identified as a reason for China's being such a small export market for South Africa's fruit and vegetable produce.

From the survey, the main products exported to the Chinese market by the respondents include the following:

1) Citrus products (including oranges, easy peelers – clementines, nartjies, etc. – and lemons)
2) Grapes and table grapes
3) Pears

---

1. The partly completed questionnaires were answers to two broad questions: a) Are you currently exporting to China? And b) If so, are you experiencing any particular problems in exporting to China?

4) Plums

(5) Wine

Even though the questionnaire was to cover fruit, vegetable and wine producers, responses from only the fruit exporting industry were obtained. In what follows, the survey response will be discussed, including the costs of doing business in China as experienced by the respondents, the NTBs to export to China, and lastly other constraints and general comments by the respondents.

5.2.1 *Generally High Phytosanitary Standards and Strict Protocols*

Strict SPS standards and high protocols on fruit quality, which are regarded as unnecessary at times by survey respondents, are the main barrier to export to China for South Africa's Western Cape fruit exporters. The strict protocols are seen as a disincentive to export to China. The lack of phytosanitary agreement between South Africa and China for specific products further inhibits exporters to the Chinese market. During President Hu Jintao's visit to South Africa in February 2007, four SPS agreements were signed. These included protocols for the export of South Africa's apples and pears to China.[1]

Similarly, in 2004 a memorandum of understanding on a sanitary and phytosanitary consultation mechanism and a protocol for phytosanitary requirements for citrus exports to China were signed.[2] However, survey respondents felt that because of the lack of a phytosanitary agreement between South Africa and China many of the shipments destined for China do not follow a direct route but are routed through Hong Kong. This has given rise to much smuggling and poses challenges for exporters that rely on legal procedures and channels. The phytosanitary import requirements create difficulties for citrus varieties to be exported to China.

5.2.2 *Logistics and Cold Sterilisation Requirements*

Official exporting channels to China require the cold treatment of fruits. This prerequisite increases the cost of the logistics chain. Generally, cold chains in fruit exports are essential, especially when products undergo long journeys. Cold sterilisation of fruit and the management thereof is vital for maintaining the freshness of the product from producer to retailer and for minimising unwanted degradation, including softening and premature ripening. Most importantly, though, cold sterilisation is required by exporting countries for entry into quarantine areas that are vulnerable to certain pests, such as fruit fly.

All citrus fruit exported from South Africa to China "must be treated by cold disinfection to mitigate fruit flies"[3]. The Western Cape, like other regions in South Africa, is home to two species of fruit fly. The potential presence of fruit fly larvae in

---

1. See http://www.dfa.gov.za/docs/2007/chin0204.htm
2. http://www.dfa.gov.za/docs/2004/chin0629.htm
3. Protocol of Phytosanitary requirements for the export of citrus fruit from South Africa to China (www.nda.agric.za).

citrus and deciduous fruit exports from the Western Cape acts as a significant non-tariff barrier for the Western Cape and other SA fruit exporters intent on penetrating stricter quarantine areas such as China.

At present, about 90 per cent of the Western Cape's deciduous fruits exports are shipped to Europe. Europe, unlike the US, Japan and China, where stricter phytosanitary measures are applied to fruit fly-infected areas, has softer phytosanitary measures. However, expected phytosanitary harmonisation will make access to markets like Europe more difficult in the future. If South Africa and specifically the Western Cape can declare fruit-producing areas fruit-fly free, cold sterilisation procedures can be relaxed, which will also enhance fruit quality. To minimise the possible jeopardy to the South African fruit industry posed by this pest, one possibility to be explored in the Western Cape is the Sterile Insect Technique (SIT) pest control programme. The isolated location of the region, and its many valleys, are expected to make implementation of this programme effective in the Western Cape.

A drawback to the cold treatment transit process, besides the increased cost of exporting and the required paperwork and data collection, is the need for fruit hardy enough to handle the cold treatment required. Overall, cold sterilisation impairs the quality of fruits, and especially of fruit that is more temperature sensitive, such as soft citrus (easy peelers). At the first port of entry into China, quarantine inspection is undertaken and full records of the cold treatment are examined. If these do not meet Chinese standards, the products will be shipped back immediately.

5.2.3 Registration of Orchards, Documentation

Any citrus fruit that originates in an unapproved orchard, production unit or packing house, storage facility or cold treatment facility is prohibited from entering China at the first port of entry. The registration process is annual and has to be approved by South Africa's Department of Agriculture. Similar processes apply to markets such as Japan.

From the survey, it became evident that Western Cape fruit exporters have identified China as a crucial market for future exports. However, the lack of support from the national government, the absence of an FTA agreement, the advantage enjoyed by major competitors that already have an established footprint in China, and the rather unnecessary and stringent SPS requirements and protocols on fruit exports (that seem to involve too many political requirements rather than objective risks), have constrained Western Cape fruit exporters in significantly penetrating the Chinese fruit market.

5.3 Comparable Overview of NTBs against Australia's Exports to China

ABARE (2006) identified the main NTBs for Australian agricultural products entering the Chinese market. These products include wool, grains, meat and other animal products, dairy, live animals and genetic material, and cotton. The findings for wool, as well as for horticulture and wine, which have been identified as potential areas for increased South African exports to China, are given below.

5.3.1 Wool

The NTB on wool imports is a tariff quota. Until 2004, two-thirds of the quota[1] was allocated to non-state trading enterprises with no quota being awarded to state trading enterprises more recently (ABARE, 2006). Traders can simply register for the application to import wool and the registered traders are awarded portions of the tariff quota. The system is based on a 'first come, first served' basis, but longer-established traders are granted larger licences than newer traders, with quota allocations revised on a yearly basis.

Wool imports are further constrained by the duplication of the inspection and classification process, resulting in higher costs of exporting wool. Australian wool exports are re-inspected and reclassified on arrival in China without regard to the testing of wool done before shipment by the Australian Wool Testing Authority.

5.3.2 Horticulture and Wine

In this category, the most significant barriers are the SPS measures, residue restrictions and food standards, which limit the pace and quantity of exports of a number of horticultural products into China. Vegetable oils used to be subject to the TRQ system[2]. Wine is also subjected to NTBs when entering the Chinese market. These include labelling specifications (labels should be in Chinese but in the original packaging), which need to be submitted for approval before the product can be traded. This process is time consuming and can take a minimum of three months. Another delay includes approval for the registration of new wine products. Further constraints have been the compositional limits proposed by the Chinese, internal taxes and distributional channels in China.

5.3.3 Meat and other Animal Products

As is the case in most other importing countries, animal-based products are subject to strict SPS measures, food safety and food standards (which include hygiene, labelling and pesticide standards), as well as specific testing and certification requirements, all of which increase the cost of exporting these products to China. The most notable measure is the zero tolerance for pathogens in raw meat imports, which, according to the US, is impossible to achieve. By contrast, the same policy is not applied to domestic meat products.

5.4 Perceived Costs of Doing Business with China

The main costs of doing business with China and key constraints for South Africa's fruit exporters in accessing the Chinese market according to the survey responses are listed in this section.

---

1. Above quota tariffs previously were at 90% and were reduced to 40% by 2004 (OECD, 2005).
2. Quotas on vegetables oil were phased out in 2006 with a tariff-only system implemented.

5.4.1 More Costly Logistics

In comparison with exports to other countries, exporting to China comes at a higher cost, both for shipping and transport and for cold chain management of the goods destined for China. Shipping lines control the export business and the general lack of price rigidity in exporting to China was a major concern. Current port facilities in South Africa were also reported as hampering trade with China. Overall, the geographical location of countries such as Australia places South Africa at a disadvantage.

5.4.2 Lack of Distribution Channels

Whereas some exporters have established their own distribution centres in China, distribution channels within the Chinese market are generally difficult to secure. This is specifically the case for wine, as there are only a few importers capable of serving the major provinces throughout the country. There is a lack in China of the local intermediaries so important if exporters are to be effective. Furthermore, a lack of understanding of the Chinese market, cultural differences and the difficulty of finding credit-worthy customers pose additional challenges for South Africa's exporters in penetrating this market. As such, local Chinese producers familiar with and having access to the main markets are the main competitors for South Africa's exporters.

5.4.3 Accreditation Period

For grape producers, accreditation is currently three-yearly. This hampers new grape growers from accessing the market, since they must wait for years to be accredited for China. Annual accreditation was suggested to enable new grape producers to enter the Chinese market more rapidly.

5.4.4 High Import Tariffs

Survey respondents indicated that one of the main reasons for the small market presence in China is the high import tariffs levied on fruit products. The most recent average tariffs on Chinese fruit imports from South Africa are shown in Table 7.

Table 9: Average tariff levied on South African fruits to China, 2007

Product	Tariff
Oranges	11%
Lemons	11%
Soft skin citrus/easy peelers	12%
Pears	12%
Plums	10%
Grapes	13%
Wine	14–65%

Source: Market Access Map (www.macmap.org)

5.4.5 More Experienced Competing Players

Players such as Australia and New Zealand have been penetrating the Chinese market for longer and are more familiar with it than South Africa is. South African exporters also find it difficult to enter the Chinese market owing to a general lack of government support. Major competitors for South Africa in China include countries with agricultural subsidies and those that have or are currently negotiating FTAs with China. The main foreign competitors in China as identified in the survey include Argentina, Australia, Chile, Egypt, Morocco, New Zealand and the United States.

5.4.6 Other Constraints

Other constraints reported include exchange rate fluctuations, tax laws and the dire prospects for proper reform, intellectual property issues (particularly trademarks), seasonality of South African products, limited trade due to bad payments and bad debt.

In the case of wine, the general palate in China is still at an early stage and, while there are some South African exporters currently exploring the growing Chinese middle class, more exciting times are seen to lie ahead.

6. Conclusions

A recent feature of world trade has been the emergence of China as a major participant as both an exporter and an importer. This phenomenon has roughly coincided with South Africa's economic and political transformation in recent years. The objective of this study is to examine the potential that China may offer to South Africa as a trading partner in this new environment, with the emphasis placed on agricultural exports from South Africa to China.

The paper covers the full stages of this relationship, from South Africa's position as provider of agricultural imports into China right through to discussing the non-tariff barriers that face South Africa's exporters in that market. This includes the results of a survey specifically undertaken for the study as well as an extensive literature review. In the paper emphasis has been placed on quantitative analysis, and the study starts by providing data from both Chinese and South Africa's official sources before moving to detailed computer models that seek to link the results from a large-scale global model through to the most detailed South African model. We emphasise that given the comprehensive nature and ambitious scope of this objective, our research is, in part, a preliminary analysis.

Overall, China has become the fifth most important destination for South Africa's exports[1], with iron ores, precious metals and stones and iron and steel related products dominating these exports. Similarly, China has moved into second place as a source of South Africa's imports, with general machinery items, electrical machinery, and clothing and footwear dominating. We also conclude that comparing and contrasting South Africa's trade data with the relevant Chinese data leaves many questions unanswered, as aspects of the trading relationship do not reconcile.

Global Chinese agricultural imports have been increasing in nominal dollars over the last ten years, but declining marginally as a percentage of total Chinese imports. Only for wool imports, the fourth main import line overall, does South Africa feature as a leading source for China. Chinese agricultural exports, while steadily increasing in nominal dollars, have been just as steadily declining as a percentage of total Chinese exports and are currently around 4 per cent of this total. Of particular interest to South Africa is the fact that the main Chinese export lines include maize and apple juice as the top two and apples in eighth place, suggesting some competitive pressures for South Africa in global markets.

South Africa's trade data confirm that wool was the main agricultural export to China during 2006, accounting for almost half of the total (US$ 31 million of a total of US$ 69 million), while sugar, fish meal and sheep skins make up much of

---

1. Although we note that this aggregated the EU into a single destination and that China is below 'destination unknown' in South African export data, as the specific destination of many precious metals is not disclosed.

the remainder. Agricultural imports from China were a greater US$ 127 million, with sausage casings (US$ 25 million) and kidney beans (US$ 22.5 million) the main import lines. It was calculated that South Africa's exporters face import tariffs of 13.96 per cent at the Chinese border while imports into South Africa face lesser tariffs of 6.79 per cent. A comparison between South Africa and New Zealand is provided to show that this fellow southern hemisphere country is doing much better overall than South Africa as an agricultural exporter into the Chinese market.

Extending the trade data analysis into a 'trade chilling' examination of products that South Africa could potentially export to China indicates that there are some but limited opportunities that may open up in the future, but both demand constraints in China and supply constraints in South Africa limit these possibilities. It is, however, noted that several of the agricultural imports into China that are currently restricted through Chinese global quotas are of particular interest to South Africa.

The results of a computer simulation exercise using the internationally accepted GTAP model are presented. These suggest that an FTA between South Africa and China would result in solid welfare gains for both partners. By 2015, South Africa's agricultural exports to China would increase by US$ 103 million, although some of this would merely be a diversion from other markets. The sectors to benefit most are 'other crops' and sugar. There is very little change in agricultural imports from China, only US$ 14 million, with half of this in beverages and tobacco products. Thus, even though an FTA provides significant gains to both partners, very few of these gains would be from the agricultural sector.

The next step is to 'drill down' further and place these results in perspective using a more disaggregated and specialised South African trade model. The first case study on the import side simulates the importation of 10,000 tons of apples from China and shows that this would potentially increase South Africa's consumption of apples by 3 per cent following a 4.2 per cent price decline on the local market.

The second case study, focusing on the regional implications within South Africa of an FTA with China, is more comprehensive and draws its initial simulation impact analysis from the GTAP results of the FTA. Although the study is a provisional and preliminary technical analysis in linking these two types of models, it nonetheless provides valuable insights. The results show some modest increases in the production of wool and horticultural crops and a small increase in sugar production. These increases are then traced through to production changes by province and detailed changes in the labour market by household profiles. While small, these changes are generally positive.

The computer analysis discussed above does not include analysis of non-tariff barriers that limit or, indeed, at times prohibit trade in many sectors. Research elsewhere has shown that these NTBs can often be significant. We provide a background to these NTBs and then review some literature on these constraints on agricultural trade with China. These barriers are pervasive.

Against this background, we undertook a dedicated survey of NTBs into China from agricultural producers in the Western Cape of South Africa. While the response was limited, it did provide a very useful preliminary analysis of what producers and exporters conceive as major problems facing exports. This survey identified China as a crucial market for future exports, but the lack of support from the national government, the absence of an FTA agreement, the advantage enjoyed by major competitors that have already established a footprint in China, and the rather unnecessary and stringent SPS requirements and protocols on fruit exports have been a constraint on significant penetration of the Chinese market by mainly Western Cape fruit exporters.

References

ABARE, 2006. *Agriculture in China: Developments and Significance for Australia.* Chapter 2. Research Report 06.2. March.

Broadman, H.G., 2007. *Africa's Silk Road: China and India's New Economic Frontier.* World Bank

Donnelly, W.A. and Manifold, D., 2005. *A Compilation of Reported Non-Tariff Measures: Description of the Information.* Office of Economics Working Paper. US International Trade Commission. May 2007, personal communication.

Jensen, H.G. and Sandrey, R., 2006. *A Possible SACU/China Free Trade Agreement (FTA): Implications for the South African Manufacturing Sector.* tralac Working Paper No. 8. Stellenbosch: US Printers.

Market Access Map, 2007. International Trade Centre, UNCTAD. [Online]. Available: www.macmap.org

Meyer, F.H. 2007. *An Application of the BFAP Sector Model.* Presentation at the 45th conference of AEASA, Fourways Johannesburg, September 2007.

Ferdinand Meyer, Cecilia Punt, Sanri Reynolds and Ron Sandrey, 2008. "Modelling the South African-China Trading Relationship", tralac Trade brief 2, January 2008.

OECD, 2005. *OECD Review of Agricultural Policies: China.* OECD Publishing, Paris.

PROVIDE, 2005. *The PROVIDE Project Standard Computable General Equilibrium Model,* Version 2. PROVIDE Technical Paper 2005:3. Western Cape Department of Agriculture, Elsenburg.

Punt, C., 2007. *The Socio-economic Impact of a Possible SACU/China Free Trade Agreement on the South African Economy. Preliminary Research Results.* PROVIDE Project, Western Cape Department of Agriculture, Elsenburg.

Reynolds, S. 2007, *Econometric Model for the South African Apple Industry.* Western Cape Department of Agriculture. Paper presented to the Agricultural Economics Association of South Africa Conference, Indaba Lodge, Johannesburg, 26-28 September.

Sandrey, R., Jensen, H.G., Vink, N. and Fundira, T., 2007. *South Africa's Way Ahead: Trade Policy Options.* tralac and University of Stellenbosch printers, Stellenbosch.

Sandrey, R. 2006a. *South African Merchandise Trade with China.* tralac Working Paper No. 3. Stellenbosch: US Printers.

Sandrey, R. 2006b. *The Trade and Economic Implications of the South African Restrictions Regime on Imports of Clothing from China.* tralac Working Paper No. 16. [Online]. Available: www.tralac.org

Sandrey, R. and Jensen, H. 2007. *Revisiting the South African-China Trading Relationship.* tralac Working Paper No. 6. [Online]. Available: www.tralac.org.

Sandrey, R. and Vink, N. 2006. *How Can South Africa Exploit New Opportunities in Agricultural Export Markets? Lessons from the New Zealand Experience.* tralac Working Paper No. 19. Stellenbosch: University of Stellenbosch Printers.

Walmsley, T.L. 2006. *A Baseline Scenario for Dynamic GTAP Model.* Revised March 2006 for the GTAP 6 Database. Center for Global Trade Analysis, Purdue University.

World Trade Atlas, 2007.

Annex A

Table A2. South African changes in imports from Chinese FTA, Shows initial tariff rates and changes in exports by $ million and percentage

	China			Botswana		Rest of SACU		ROW		total	
	AVE * tariff	change in value mill US$	% change quantity of imports	change in value mill US$	% change quantity of imports	change in value mill US$	% change quantity of imports	change in value mill US$	% change quantity of imports	change in value mill US$	% change quantity of imports
Primary											
1 pdr	0.0	0	0	0	-1.5	0	-0.5	0	1.1	0	0.8
2 wht	2.0	0	20	0	0.0	0	0.2	1	0.8	1	0.8
3 gro	29.5	0	97	0	0.1	0	0.5	0	0.6	0	0.7
4 v_f	9.9	3	39	0	-2.9	0	-1.9	-1	-1.9	1	1.5
5 osd	0.5	0	3	0	-0.1	0	0.1	0	0.9	0	0.8
6 c_b	20.0	0	171	0	0.3	0	1.1	0	1.5	0	5.7
7 pfb	14.1	0	93	0	-0.6	0	1.1	2	0.3	0	0.4
8 ocr	11.5	2	104	0	-0.9	0	0.0	2	0.6	4	1.5
9 ctl	0.0	0	0	0	-0.3	0	0.1	0	0.3	0	0.1
10 oap	0.3	0	2	0	0.6	0	0.6	1	1.0	1	1.0
11 rmk	0.0	0	0	0	-1.5	0	0.4	0	1.1	0	1.1
12 wol	2.1	0	33	0	-0.7	0	1.3	0	1.7	0	1.7
		5		0		0		4		9	
Secondary											
17 cmt	22.3	0		0	-0.8	0	-0.1	0	0.2	0	0.0
18 omt	8.2	1		0	-0.6	0	-0.8	0	-0.1	1	0.7
19 vol	10.5	0		0	-0.6	0	0.4	0	0.2	1	0.3
20 mil	0.0	0		0	0.3	0	0.5	0	0.3	0	0.3
21 pcr	0.0	0		0	5.9	0	0.8	0	0.1	0	0.2
22 sgr	0.0	0		0	1.3	0	0.5	1	0.7	1	0.6
23 ofd	6.7	1		0	0.7	0	0.2	1	0.2	2	0.4
24 b_t	42.8	6		0	-1.7	-1	-1.9	-3	-2.2	3	1.6
		9		0		0		-1		8	
		1,578		-12		-32		-1,005		529	

Annex A

Table A2, South African changes in imports from Chinese FTA, Shows initial tariff rates and changes in exports by $ million and percentage

	China			Botswana		Rest of SACU		ROW		total	
	AVE* tariff	change in value mill US$	% change quantity of imports	change in value mill US$	% change quantity of imports	change in value mill US$	% change quantity of imports	change in value mill US$	% change quantity of imports	change in value mill US$	% change quantity of imports
Primary											
1 pdr	0.0	0	0	0	-1.5	0	-0.5	0	1.1	0	0.8
2 wht	2.0	0	20	0	0.0	0	0.2	1	0.8	1	0.8
3 gro	29.5	0	97	0	0.1	0	0.5	0	0.6	0	0.7
4 v_f	9.9	3	39	0	-2.9	0	-1.9	-1	-1.9	1	1.5
5 osd	0.5	0	3	0	-0.1	0	0.1	0	0.9	0	0.8
6 c_b	20.0	0	171	0	0.3	0	1.1	0	1.5	0	5.7
7 pfb	14.1	0	93	0	-0.6	0	1.1	0	0.3	4	0.4
8 ocr	11.5	2	104	0	-0.9	0	0.0	2	0.6	0	1.5
9 ctl	0.0	0	0	0	-0.3	0	0.1	0	0.3	1	0.1
10 oap	0.3	0	2	0	0.6	0	0.6	1	1.0	0	1.0
11 rmk	0.0	0	0	0	-1.5	0	0.4	0	1.1	0	1.1
12 wol	2.1	0	33	0	-0.7	0	1.3	0	1.7	0	1.7
		5	9	0		0		4		9	
Secondary											
17 cmt	22.3	0		0	-0.8	0	-0.1	0	0.2	0	0.0
18 omt	8.2	1		0	-0.6	0	-0.8	0	-0.1	1	0.7
19 vol	10.5	0		0	-0.6	0	0.4	0	0.2	1	0.3
20 mil	0.0	0		0	0.3	0	0.5	0	0.3	0	0.3
21 pcr	0.0	0		0	5.9	0	0.8	0	0.1	0	0.2
22 sgr	0.0	0		0	1.3	0	0.5	1	0.7	1	0.6
23 ofd	6.7	1		0	0.7	0	0.2	1	0.2	2	0.4
24 b_t	42.8	6		0	-1.7	-1	-1.9	-3	-2.2	3	1.6
		9		0		-1		-1		8	
		1,578		-12		-32		-1,005		529	

51

Annex B

South Africa's agricultural trade relationship with China:
The Potential Implications

**A Survey of Western Cape Agricultural producers to evaluate
the barriers to trade in exporting to China**

Centre for Chinese Studies
University of Stellenbosch

August 2007

CENTRE FOR
CHINESE STUDIES

20th August 2007

Dear Sir/ Madam

Re: Request for participation in Agricultural Survey

I trust this note finds you well.

The Centre for Chinese Studies (CCS), at Stellenbosch University in cooperation with the Trade Law Centre of Southern Africa (tralac), at Stellenbosch University, is currently undertaking a research project entitled: *South Africa's agricultural trade relationship with China: The Potential Implications.*

The project, funded by the Nordic Africa Institute in Sweden explores the South Africa-China agricultural trading relationship. The overall aim of this study is to evaluate where the lines of complementarity and divergence lie between China and South Africa as regards to market share in the agricultural sector. The study will explore what China may mean for South African agricultural exports in the future. Furthermore, the project is also a pilot study for a broader study to be undertaken.

In light of the above the Centre for Chinese Studies would appreciate your time in filling out the brief survey attached. We would like to thank you for your considered attention. Please do not hesitate to contact me for any clarification regarding the research project.

We look forward to your participation in this matter and trust to receive your response by 3rd September 2007.

Sincerely yours

Hannah Edinger
Research Manager
Centre for Chinese Studies
University of Stellenbosch

T +27 21 808 2840
F +27 21 808 2841
M +27 72 198 3335
E hedinger@sun.ac.za
W www.ccs.org.za

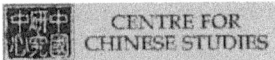

CENTRE FOR
CHINESE STUDIES

Profile of the Centre for Chinese Studies
Stellenbosch University

The Centre for Chinese Studies (CCS) is the first institution devoted to the study of China on the African continent. The CCS promotes the exchange of knowledge, ideas and experiences between China and Africa. As Africa's interaction with China increases, the need for greater analysis and understanding between our two regions and peoples grows. The Centre seeks to fulfill this role.

Housed at Stellenbosch University in the Western Cape Province, the CCS is a joint undertaking between the Governments of South Africa and the People's Republic of China having been agreed to at the South Africa-PRC Bi-national Commission held in June 2004. The Centre conducts analysis of China-related research to stakeholders in Government, business, academia and NGO communities. We are also active delivering lectures to academic and business audiences both locally and internationally.

The Centre is active in delivering business strategy content to academic and business audiences at the Graduate School of Business at Stellenbosch University, as well as private sector corporates. The CCS also forms part of the African Economic Research Consortium's Asian Driver Programme which seeks to investigate China and India's developmental impact on the African continent.

The CCS hosts visiting academics and Government officials within the China Forum that provides a platform for discussion and debate on China-Africa related subjects. China Forum events are often hosted in collaboration with other institutions.

The CCS has co-operative linkages with key Chinese universities and institutions pursuing both research collaboration and exchange undertakings. These linkages include Beijing University and the Chinese Academy of Social Sciences.

The Centre for Chinese Studies is also home to the Confucius Institute, the first of its kind in South Africa. Through the Confucius Institute, the CCS is projecting Chinese language and cultural studies in the Africa region. The CCS thus serves as the foremost knowledge bridge between China and the African continent.

Centre for Chinese Studies
Stellenbosch University

T +27 21 808 2840
F +27 21 808 2841
E ccsinfo@sun.ac.za
W www.ccs.org.za

CENTRE FOR CHINESE STUDIES

The Centre for Chinese Studies
in cooperation with the
Trade Law Centre for Southern Africa

A Survey of Western Cape Agricultural producers to evaluate the barriers to trade in exporting to China

Thank you for taking the time to fill out this short questionnaire. Please write your response in the space provided, or if options are provided, please tick the most applicable option.

A.	GENERAL INFORMATION

City/District

Company Name

The purpose of this survey is to gather information on the barriers that South African producers in the fruit and vegetable sector (in the Western Cape) face in accessing and exporting to the Chinese agricultural market.

B.	QUESTIONNAIRE

Q 1	What products do you produce, which of these products are exported and to what markets are these exported to?

Products:	% of product exported	Main market for export	% share	Chinese market share %
1.				
2.				
3.				
4.				
5.				
6.				
7.				
8.				
9.				
10.				

Q 2	If your company is not exporting to China, what would you say the reason for this is?

Please specify: _____
_____
_____
_____

Q 3	Do you see China as a future market for your product/s?

Yes	
No	

Q 4	Who would you say are your main competitors in China?

Main competitors in China:
1.
2.
3.
4.
5.

Q 5	What sort of an advantage, if any, would you say your competitors in China have?

Advantages of competitors
1.
2.
3.
4.
5.

Q 6	What are the costs of doing business with China over and above the "normal" costs of doing business? *For example: Would you suggest that it is more difficult to market your product in the Chinese market than elsewhere?*

Costs of doing business in China:
1.
2.
3.

Q 7	What sort of non-tariff barriers (NTBs) would you identify that restrict your product's entry into China?

Non-tariff barriers as constraints:
1.
2.
3.
4.
5.

Q 8	What are your main constraints in accessing the Chinese market?

Constraints to access Chinese market:
1.
2.
3.
4.
5.

Q 9	Generally, what barriers to export does your firm face (not only to China)?

General export barriers:
1.
2.
3.
4.
5.

C. OPTIONAL

If you would like to note any additional comments about your experiences from any dealings/ interactions you may have had with exporting your produce to China, please add these below.

_____
_____
_____
_____
_____
_____
_____
_____
_____
_____
_____
_____
_____
_____
_____
_____
_____
_____
_____
_____
_____
_____
_____

THIS IS THE END OF THE QUESTIONNAIRE

THANK YOU VERY MUCH FOR PARTICIPATING IN OUR RESEARCH

Should you wish to discuss this topic further and are willing to take part in any further research the Centre for Chinese Studies pursues on this topic please could you specify your contact details below.

Name: _____

Position: _____

Company: _____

Contact Details: _____

_____

_____

_____

DISCUSSION PAPERS PUBLISHED BY THE INSTITUTE

Recent issues in the series are available electronically for downloading free of charge

www.nai.uu.se

1. Kenneth Hermele and Bertil Odén, *Sanctions and Dilemmas. Some Implications of Economic Sanctions against South Africa*. 1988. 43 pp. ISBN 91-7106-286-6

2. Elling Njål Tjønneland, *Pax Pretoriana. The Fall of Apartheid and the Politics of Regional Destabilisation*. 1989. 31 pp. ISBN 91-7106-292-0

3. Hans Gustafsson, Bertil Odén and Andreas Tegen, *South African Minerals. An Analysis of Western Dependence*. 1990. 47 pp. ISBN 91-7106-307-2

4. Bertil Egerö, *South African Bantustans. From Dumping Grounds to Battlefronts*. 1991. 46 pp. ISBN 91-7106-315-3

5. Carlos Lopes, *Enough is Enough! For an Alternative Diagnosis of the African Crisis*. 1994. 38 pp. ISBN 91-7106-347-1

6. Annika Dahlberg, *Contesting Views and Changing Paradigms*. 1994. 59 pp. ISBN 91-7106-357-9,

7. Bertil Odén, *Southern African Futures. Critical Factors for Regional Development in Southern Africa*. 1996. 35 pp. ISBN 91-7106-392-7

8. Colin Leys and Mahmood Mamdani, *Crisis and Reconstruction – African Perspectives*. 1997. 26 pp. ISBN 91-7106-417-6

9. Gudrun Dahl, *Responsibility and Partnership in Swedish Aid Discourse*. 2001. 30 pp. ISBN 91-7106-473-7

10. Henning Melber and Christopher Saunders, *Transition in Southern Africa – Comparative Aspects*. 2001. 28 pp. ISBN 91-7106-480-X

11. *Regionalism and Regional Integration in Africa*. 2001. 74 pp. ISBN 91-7106-484-2

12. Souleymane Bachir Diagne, et al., *Identity and Beyond: Rethinking Africanity*. 2001. 33 pp. ISBN 91-7106-487-7

13. Georges Nzongola-Ntalaja, et al., *Africa in the New Millennium*. Edited by Raymond Suttner. 2001. 53 pp. ISBN 91-7106-488-5

14. *Zimbabwe's Presidential Elections 2002*. Edited by Henning Melber. 2002. 88 pp. ISBN 91-7106-490-7

15. Birgit Brock-Utne, *Language, Education and Democracy in Africa*. 2002. 47 pp. ISBN 91-7106-491-5

16. Henning Melber et al., *The New Partnership for Africa's development (NEPAD)*. 2002. 36 pp. ISBN 91-7106-492-3

17. Juma Okuku, *Ethnicity, State Power and the Democratisation Process in Uganda*. 2002. 42 pp. ISBN 91-7106-493-1

18. Yul Derek Davids, et al., *Measuring Democracy and Human Rights in Southern Africa*. Compiled by Henning Melber. 2002. 50 pp. ISBN 91-7106-497-4

19. Michael Neocosmos, Raymond Suttner and Ian Taylor, *Political Cultures in Democratic South Africa*. Compiled by Henning Melber. 2002. 52 pp. ISBN 91-7106-498-2

20. Martin Legassick, *Armed Struggle and Democracy. The Case of South Africa*. 2002. 53 pp. ISBN 91-7106-504-0

21. Reinhart Kössler, Henning Melber and Per Strand, *Development from Below. A Namibian Case Study*. 2003. 32 pp. ISBN 91-7106-507-5

22. Fred Hendricks, *Fault-Lines in South African Democracy. Continuing Crises of Inequality and Injustice*. 2003. 32 pp. ISBN 91-7106-508-3

23. Kenneth Good, *Bushmen and Diamonds. (Un)Civil Society in Botswana*. 2003. 39 pp. ISBN 91-7106-520-2

24. Robert Kappel, Andreas Mehler, Henning Melber and Anders Danielson, *Structural Stability in an African Context*. 2003. 55 pp. ISBN 91-7106-521-0

25. Patrick Bond, *South Africa and Global Apartheid. Continental and International Policies and Politics*. 2004. 45 pp. ISBN 91-7106-523-7

26. Bonnie Campbell (ed.), *Regulating Mining in Africa. For whose benefit?* 2004. 89 pp. ISBN 91-7106-527-X

27. Suzanne Dansereau and Mario Zamponi, *Zimbabwe – The Political Economy of Decline.* Compiled by Henning Melber. 2005. 43 pp. ISBN 91-7106-541-5

28. Lars Buur and Helene Maria Kyed, *State Recognition of Traditional Authority in Mozambique. The nexus of Community Representation and State Assistance.* 2005. 30 pp. ISBN 91-7106-547-4

29. Hans Eriksson and Björn Hagströmer, *Chad – Towards Democratisation or Petro-Dictatorship?* 2005. 82 pp. ISBN 91-7106-549-0

30. Mai Palmberg and Ranka Primorac (eds), *Skinning the Skunk – Facing Zimbabwean Futures.* 2005. 40 pp. ISBN 91-7106-552-0

31. Michael Brüntrup, Henning Melber and Ian Taylor, *Africa, Regional Cooperation and the World Market – Socio-Economic Strategies in Times of Global Trade Regimes.* Compiled by Henning Melber. 2006. 70 pp. ISBN 91-7106-559-8

32. Fibian Kavulani Lukalo, *Extended Handshake or Wrestling Match? – Youth and Urban Culture Celebrating Politics in Kenya.* 2006. 58 pp. ISBN 91-7106-567-9

33. Tekeste Negash, *Education in Ethiopia: From Crisis to the Brink of Collapse.* 2006. 55 pp. ISBN 91-7106-576-8

34. Fredrik Söderbaum and Ian Taylor (eds) *Micro-Regionalism in West Africa. Evidence from Two Case Studies.* 2006. 32 pp. ISBN 91-7106-584-9

35. Henning Melber (ed.), *On Africa – Scholars and African Studies.* 2006. 68 pp. ISBN 978-91-7106-585-8

36. Amadu Sesay, *Does One Size Fit All? The Sierra Leone Truth and Reconciliation Commission Revisited.* 2007. 56 pp. ISBN 978-91-7106-586-5

37. Karolina Hulterström, Amin Y. Kamete and Henning Melber, *Political Opposition in African Countries – The Case of Kenya, Namibia, Zambia and Zimbabwe.* 2007. 86 pp. ISBN 978-7106-587-2

38. Henning Melber (ed.), *Governance and State Delivery in Southern Africa. Examples from Botswana, Namibia and Zimbabwe.* 2007. 65 pp. ISBN 978-91-7106-587-2

39. Cyril Obi (ed.), *Perspectives on Côte d'Ivoire: Between Political Breakdown and Post-Conflict Peace.* 2007. 66 pp. ISBN 978-91-7106-606-6

40. Anna Chitando, *Imagining a Peaceful Society. A Vision of Children's Literature in a Post-Conflict Zimbabwe.* 2008. 26 pp. ISBN 978-91-7106-623-7

41. Olawale Ismail, *The Dynamics of Post-Conflict Reconstruction and Peace Building in West Africa. Between Change and Stability.* 2009. 52 pp. ISBN 978-91-7106-637-4

42. Ron Sandrey and Hannah Edinger, *Examining the South Africa–China Agricultural Relationship.* 2009. 58 pp. ISBN 978-91-7106-643-5

www.ingramcontent.com/pod-product-compliance
Lightning Source LLC
Chambersburg PA
CBHW080056280326
41934CB00014B/3333